SCARED STIFF

SCARED STIFF

EVERYTHING YOU NEED TO KNOW ABOUT
50 FAMOUS PHOBIAS

Sara Latta

Foreword by Elizabeth McMahon, PhD

35 Stillman Street, Suite 121
San Francisco, CA 94107
www.zestbooks.net

Young Adult Nonfiction / Social Science/Psychology
Library of Congress control number: 2013918451
ISBN: 978-1-936976-49-2

Cover design: Dagmar Trojanek
Interior design: Tanya Napier

Manufactured in the U.S.A.
DOC 10 9 8 7 6 5 4 3 2 1
4500452649

Connect with Zest!

zestbooks.net/blog
zestbooks.net/contests
twitter.com/zestbooks
facebook.com/zestbook
facebook.com/BooksWithATwist
pinterest.com/zestbooks

ACKNOWLEDGMENTS

Many thanks to the people at Zest Books, especially Daniel Harmon, who believed I could write about phobias and waited patiently to find out whether he was right, and Jeff Campbell, who asked all the right questions and made my words shine.

Thanks to my husband Tony Liss, who stands with me at each dizzying precipice and helps me turn each fear into a challenge.

DEDICATION

To those who are afraid of things that go bump in the night, of high places and tight spaces, of things that slither and words that hurt: You are not alone.

TABLE OF CONTENTS

APPENDIX

FOREWORD

I vividly remember one hot East Coast summer when I was about thirteen years old. My younger sisters, my parents, and I were at the swimming pool. I was frozen with fear as I tried to take that first, tiny dive off the side into the water only inches below. Kneeling close to the water, arms poised, I felt paralyzed with fear, literally scared stiff; while, to my intense embarrassment, my (much younger!) sisters were diving into the water with carefree abandon. How can the same thing be so frightening to one person and so exhilarating to someone else?

Why do some people love to jump out of planes with nothing more than a parachute, while other people are too scared to even take a one-hour flight to a great vacation spot? Why do some people have reptiles as pets, while other people can't even bear to read the word "s-n-a-k-e"? How can something so innocuous trigger such an intense attack of fear and terror?

This much-needed book provides answers to all those questions and more. Enjoy the ride as Sara Latta takes you on an entertaining and informative tour of the most interesting and well-known phobias from acrophobia (fear of heights) to wiccaphobia (fear of witches). Phobias are not just a minor nuisance. They can keep you from activities and experiences that are important parts of growing into a successful and happy adult. For example, fear of social situations can make it hard to make friends, go on dates, or enjoy parties. Students with topophobia (fear of speaking or otherwise performing in public) can drop out of school or refuse to go to college just to get out of having to speak up in class. According to statistics from the National Institute of Mental Health (NIMH), fear of public speaking is the most common phobia, with nearly three out of every four people (74 percent) surveyed saying they have this fear. Fear of public speaking has actually ranked higher than fear of dying in many such studies. "I'd rather die than have to get up on stage and give a speech" actually reflects how a lot of people feel.

The NIMH reports that as of August 2012, 6.3 million Americans have a diagnosed phobia. And, in all likelihood, there are uncounted millions more who are struggling with phobias but haven't yet been diagnosed. Although phobias can develop at any age, starting in early childhood, many commonly appear in the teen years, between fifteen to twenty years old.

The situation is far from hopeless, however. As a clinical psychologist, one of my specialties is treating anxiety problems like phobias. Phobias and the panic they create became a special interest of mine because I kept seeing research studies showing that treatment is really effective. I love seeing people with problems that can be treated! I'm not saying overcoming a phobia is always easy or pleasant, but if you have a phobia, you can get over it.

But this still begs the question of why this capacity for terror has been hardwired into our brains? Well, it's probably because fear and the fight-or-flight response it triggers are life-saving when we are in danger. Some fears even seem to be present from birth, such as the fear of falling, which infants demonstrate before they are even old enough to walk or talk.

But what makes a fear a phobia? And why do phobias have such bizarrely unpronounceable names (like triskaidekaphobia)? Using her skill as a science writer, Sara Latta makes the whole topic of phobias fun to read about and easy to understand. She explains the difference between a reality-based fear (like the fear of climbing a mountain in a thunderstorm) and an actual phobia (like the utter inability to take so much as a step on a sturdy ladder). Here, you'll find references to phobia-related movie scenes, phobia quotes, and inside information about famous people with phobias. Once you start reading, you won't want to stop.

Perhaps one of the most frustrating and embarrassing aspects of a phobia is that your level of fear has nothing to do with the actual amount of danger you face. Many phobics realize this intellectually, but still can't overcome their physical and emotional reactions. Just the thought of your phobia may be enough to trigger an intense feeling of fear. It does not matter how smart, mature, talented, or successful you are; you can still find yourself terrified by an irrational fear. So one of the most important questions is, once you have a phobia, how can you get over it?

In *Scared Stiff*, you will learn about several proven approaches to successfully overcoming phobias. You will read how and why these techniques for treating fears work. You will even learn about one of the newest, most exciting advances in treating fears: Virtual Reality Therapy (VRT). And, as it happens, this is an area of particular interest to me. Helping people get over their fear is so satisfying that I have happily spent much of my career focusing on it—and VRT represents the state of the art in this endeavor.

VRT is available for four of the most widespread phobias: fear of public speaking (topophobia), fear of heights (acrophobia), fear of flying (aviophobia), and fear of thunderstorms (astraphobia). VRT lets you "face" your fear in a controlled virtual environment so you can overcome your phobia in small, gradual steps. Decreased fear in the virtual environment carries over to the real world. I have helped hundreds of people overcome their phobias using the cognitive and behavioral therapies described in the book, and a few years ago, I began using VRT as well. My experience is that VRT is extremely effective in treating these phobias and makes treatment faster and easier.

Whether you're looking for information, perspective, or just a fun anecdote, this book has you covered. And, no matter what your fear may be, by the end of this book, you are likely to know more about it. You will learn about what phobias are, who has them, and what to do about them. So read on to become a font of fun phobia facts and an expert on the topic of terror.

And, by the way, I did eventually teach myself to dive!

—Elizabeth McMahon, PhD

INTRODUCTION
PHOBIAS 101

Does the mere thought of speaking in public leave you in a cold sweat? Do you freak when you see a spider? Well, you're not the only one. Fear is an important survival mechanism that helps protect us from danger. Most people manage to control their fears and get on with their daily lives. They forge ahead with their oral presentations; they breathe deep and brush away the spider webs. But for some people, these fears are not so easily dismissed. For some people, these fears are overwhelming, paralyzing, and apparently indomitable.

Personally, my biggest fear is heights (probably because I'm kind of a klutz: I once injured myself by literally falling off a log). But I was able to put my fear aside for long enough to climb up (and then down, which is far scarier) several very high and steep pyramids in Mexico, because the view was great and I wanted bragging rights. As a result, it's pretty clear that although I may have a fear of high places, I'm certainly not phobic when it comes to heights. For some, however, the very idea of possibly encountering a spider, going to school, or using a public restroom can be so terrifying that they can't go about their everyday lives.

Normal, garden-variety fear becomes a phobia only when it is persistent, excessive, and unreasonable. People with phobias will do just about anything to avoid the places, situations, or things that frighten them—even when they *know* there's no real threat of danger. When those irrational fears cause problems, they become phobias. If you fear zombies, you may want to avoid reading or watching *World War Z*, but your fear doesn't become a phobia unless it interferes with your ability to function as an extra in a zombie movie (or a similarly secure environment).

Psychiatrists put phobias into three categories. A specific phobia is the extreme fear of an object, situation, or experience. Some examples of specific phobias are fear of flying, fear of dogs, or fear of being in closed-in spaces. People with social phobias are very anxious about being embarrassed, mocked, or criticized by others. People with this disorder, also called social anxiety disorder, often feel extremely anxious in all social situations. They may avoid going to parties, speaking in public, or meeting new people. (And although it is similar to shyness in many respects, the intensity of this feeling is quite different.) In some cases, social phobias may be triggered by an actual social situation, but that is not always the case. Agoraphobia may be the most crippling phobia type of all. Agoraphobics fear having a panic attack in a place or situation from which escape would be difficult or embarrassing. It's not the situation that frightens them so much as it is the fear of the panic attack itself. People with this disorder may come to feel they cannot leave their homes.

IT'S ALL GREEK TO ME...

The word *phobia* comes from the Greek word *phóbos*, meaning "fear" or "terror." Phobos was the name of a god who had the job of scaring the crap out of the enemies of the Greeks. He certainly *sounds* scary; those who worshipped Phobos often made bloody sacrifices in his name, and warriors carried shields with his image, "staring backwards with eyes that glowed with fire. His mouth was full of teeth in a white row, fearful and daunting." Intense!

Hippocrates (460–377 BC) was among the first to describe someone with phobias: "He would not go near a precipice, or over a bridge or beside even the shallowest ditch, and yet he could walk in the ditch itself . . . When he used to begin drinking, the girl flute-player would frighten him; as soon as he heard the first note of the flute at a banquet, he would be beset by terror."

Many phobias are deeply rooted in superstitions so common they hold sway over entire cultures and communities. Triskaidekaphobia, the fear of the number 13, for example, is rooted in an ancient belief that the number is unlucky. Superstition-based phobias often become social norms—so much so that people take them for granted. Some older buildings lack a thirteenth floor, for example, because many cultures associate the number with bad luck. Historically, people thought some of the more quirky phobias were caused by the usual scapegoats: witches, demons, or evil spirits. Today, we're starting to get a pretty good idea of why some people develop phobias. But while they can *feel* like a curse, they have more to do with brain chemistry than with malevolent beings.

THE HOME OF FEAR

Fear's home base is the amygdalae, two little almond-shaped nuggets on either side of the brain. When you see or hear something scary—a hissing snake, say—that information flies to the amygdalae, which store memories of emotions, including fear. Trigger the amygdalae, and terror kicks in. It's the brain's early warning system. Danger! Do something, quick!

But that same information also travels to the reasoning part of your brain, the prefrontal cortex, which then passes it on to the amygdalae. It can tell the amygdalae, "Relax, silly, it's only a garter snake." Thus, over time, the brain learns to squash many of our potential fear triggers. (Of course, in the case of real danger, the message is different: "You are so totally right! It's a coral snake!")

Scientists have found that the connection between the prefrontal cortex and the amygdalae is weaker in people who suffer from anxiety disorders, including phobias. For some reason, in these people the amygdalae just don't get the memo that there's nothing to fear; they just keep blaring their warning sirens to the rest of the body. What's more, teenage brains seem to have a harder time than those of children or adults turning off the amygdalae's fear response. This might explain why anxiety disorders seem to spike during or just before adolescence.

Whether the trigger is a spider or your friendly dentist, the symptoms of different phobias are similar: feelings of dread or terror, sweating, nausea, a pounding heartbeat, trembling, screaming or crying, even anger. It's the classic "fight or flight" response: Get ready to do battle or run like heck. Phobias can sometimes trigger feelings of such intense panic that sufferers feel as though they are having a heart attack. The physical symptoms of anxiety and panic are bad enough, but sufferers often feel as though they are going crazy. But it's important to remember that neither you nor the millions of other people who suffer from severe anxiety or panic attacks are crazy. Instead, you have a condition that is, fortunately, often very treatable. At the end of this book there's even a special section devoted to facing—and overcoming—many of the most common phobias.

EVOLUTION AND CULTURE

It's no coincidence that many specific phobias fall into one of four categories: fear of blood or injury, fear of insects and animals, fear of the natural environment, and fear of dangerous situations. All of these reflect fears that have helped the human species to survive. Evolutionary psychologists argue that we are hardwired to react to the threats faced by our Stone Age ancestors. Today, cars kill far more people than spiders, but there are not many people with car phobias. Evolution theory tells us that our anxieties just haven't had time to adapt to the modern age.

But fears also get passed down from one generation to the next. "Sleep tight; don't let the bedbugs bite" may seem harmless enough, but it reinforces the notion that insects are to be feared (although bedbugs themselves are no picnic). A child might well develop a phobia of dogs, for example, if his parents show that they are afraid of dogs. And as if it weren't already easy enough to develop these phobias, we now have to deal with the phobia-reinforcing machine that is the media today. Television, movies, books, music, and the internet all do their part to hone in on and play off of our fears—whether based in reality, or bred in our imagination, or lying somewhere in between.

FAUX PHOBIAS

The suffix of phobia isn't always used in a strictly technical way. *Xenophobia*, for instance, (from the Greek word *xenos*, meaning "stranger" or "foreigner"), is used most commonly to denote what is essentially extreme prejudice toward groups of people viewed as "different" or "other." Most babies begin to show a fear of individual strangers by around seven to nine months. Typically, however, they outgrow their fear as they become exposed to more strangers and learn that most of them can be pretty nice people.

Adult xenophobia is not so innocent. It has been the basis for much of the evil that groups of people inflict upon one another. There is often some overlap between xenophobia and racism, but they're not the same thing. Racism is the belief that people with one set of physical characteristics that we've come to think of as defining race—skin color, hair type, facial features—are somehow superior to those who don't share those attributes. Xenophobia, on the other hand, is based on the prejudice that certain groups of people are outsiders or foreign and therefore not truly a part of the community or nation.

Xenophobia

Psychologists believe that babies' fear of strangers begins to arise around the time that they are able to remember and recognize the familiar features of their parents, who they associate with food, warmth, and love. When babies are confronted with an unfamiliar face, it can suddenly become very scary! This may have evolutionary roots: Baby chimpanzees, for example, begin to fear strangers at about the same time as human infants—probably linked to the danger of raids from neighboring bands of apes.

The adult fear of strangers or foreigners may also be traced to our ancient ancestors. Villagers may have had cause to fear that invading tribes would swoop in, burn down their huts and steal their food, and rape their women. Other fears may be related to feelings of disgust: "Ugh! Anybody who eats snails (substitute: horsemeat, mealworms, bull testicles, squirrels, you name it) is not to be trusted!"

But again, when a natural distrust grows into irrational fear and hatred, it becomes xenophobia. This ugly phobia is on the rise worldwide, accompanied by alarming increases in violence and discrimination. There are several reasons to explain the rise in xenophobia. First of all, we just move around a lot more than we used to. New immigrants bring with them different beliefs or cultural traditions. For some people, the unfamiliar is frightening, and they treat newcomers with suspicion and even hatred. This is especially true in times of national crisis. When the Japanese attacked Pearl Harbor and the US entered World War II, Japanese migrants and Japanese-Americans living on the West Coast were sent to internment camps. Japanophobia, aided by government propaganda, became widespread. Something similar is happening today, in the aftermath of the 9/11 attacks. Islamophobia—the prejudice and irrational fear of all Muslims—is on the rise, resulting in hate crimes and discrimination. That hatred has even spilled over against people who look or dress differently, even though they may not be Muslim.

In tough economic times, some people fear that immigrants will take away jobs or use up scarce public services. Sociologists have concluded that some of the arguments against illegal immigration are rooted in xenophobia and Hispanophobia (fear of Hispanics).

Homophobia (fear of homosexuals), gerontophobia (fear of elderly people), and psychophobia (fear of the mentally ill) are all examples of so-called phobias that are more properly called prejudice.

There is a famous comedy routine from the 1960s in which Carl Reiner plays a journalist interviewing Mel Brooks, the 2,000-Year-Old Man. Brooks recalls the early days, singing his cave's national anthem: "Let 'Em All Go to Hell, Except Cave Seventy-Six."

The 2,000-Year-Old Man had it figured out: We all think our own cave, with its particular values and beliefs, is the very best. This idea is funny until it turns into xenophobia.

TURN XENOPHOBIA ON ITS HEAD...

. . . and you get oikophobia: the fear of home surroundings (the term is from the Greek word *oikos*, meaning "household"). In the early nineteenth century, the word *oikophobia* was used to describe a desire to leave home and travel. It became, essentially, a synonym for *wanderlust*. In recent years, some conservative writers have adopted the word to describe liberals whom they believe take the side of "them" versus "us."

A FINAL WORD

In *Scared Stiff,* we'll take a look at 50 phobias that freak us out, from acrophobia (fear of heights) to wiccaphobia (fear of witches). The people, things, and situations that frighten us are just about as diverse as life—or rather, the human imagination itself—and include things like animals (fear of bugs), the natural environment (water), situations (flying), medical procedures (needles), or just random objects (buttons). We'll visit some of the most common social phobias as well, including the fear of going to school or speaking in public. The fear of having a panic attack in a public situation, agoraphobia, is in a category all its own. You'll learn about each phobia (including the sometimes baffling origin of their names), as well as how and why it develops and how it has been represented (and sometimes distorted) by pop culture. So you'll be able to impress your friends not only with interesting scientific facts, but also with your in-depth knowledge of famous phobics and famous fears in films. Last of all, you'll get some advice about how to overcome these phobias and where to seek additional help. So without further ado, let's get to it—and start to face our fears!

SCARE QUOTES

"Racism, xenophobia, and unfair discrimination have spawned slavery, when human beings have bought and sold and owned and branded fellow human beings as if they were so many beasts of burden."
—Bishop Desmond Tutu

"The oldest and strongest emotion of mankind is fear, and the oldest and strongest kind of fear is fear of the unknown."
—H. P. Lovecraft

"I do not believe from what I have been told about this people, that there is anything barbarous or savage about them, except that we all call barbarous anything that is contrary to our own habits."
—Sixteenth-century writer Michel de Montaigne, commenting in his essay "On Cannibals" on his encounter in France with a Brazilian native

"Remember, remember always that all of us, and you and I especially, are descended from immigrants and revolutionists."
—Franklin D. Roosevelt

ACROPHOBIA

FEAR OF HEIGHTS

Fear of heights is one of the most common phobias, as it's related to the very understandable (and healthy) fear of falling. The name itself is derived from the Greek word *ákron*, meaning "peak," "summit," or "edge." Most people have some fear of heights, at least under certain circumstances (such as standing at the edge of the Grand Canyon), but as with all fears, it becomes a phobia when the reaction is so extreme or persistent that it interferes with everyday life. People with acrophobia might become very anxious and dizzy just thinking about being in a high place, and if they found themselves high above the ground, they might freeze and be unable to move or get down safely without help.

The fear of heights is a basic survival mechanism. Even babies have a fear of falling. One scientific study found babies will refuse to crawl across a sturdy but clear Plexiglas surface—even if their mothers are beckoning them to come.

Of course, babies and children *do* fall as they learn to walk, and the memory of that experience may be what results in fear of heights. Then again, not everyone has a good sense of balance, and someone's fear of heights might relate to that; either consciously or subconsciously, they don't trust themselves when there is a danger of falling.

Balance depends on three body systems working together. Fluid-filled loops lined with tiny hairlike nerve endings in the inner ear provide information about our head's movement. Then, pressure receptors in our muscles give us the ability to know where a body part is in space; this allows us to walk up a flight of stairs without having to look at each step. We also use visual cues to help us figure out where we are and how we are moving. Have you ever been in one of those crazy tilt houses where water appears to run uphill and everyone seems to lean at odd angles? These structures trick our eyes by mixing up our visual cues, which can affect our sense of balance while we're in them.

Scientists have found that people with a fear of heights may rely on vision more than other people to keep their balance. They balance fine on the ground, but when they have to cross a narrow bridge, for example, the familiar visual cues are suddenly very far away. If they have trouble maintaining their balance using their body's internal mechanisms, they may begin to sway back and forth—which of course makes their situation truly dangerous. So, it would make sense for them to avoid these situations.

AT THE MOVIES

Film director and producer Alfred Hitchcock made acrophobia a central plot point in his classic movie *Vertigo*, starring James Stewart and Kim Novak. Stewart plays a detective (nicknamed Scottie) whose acrophobia results in the death of a fellow police officer after a rooftop chase. Scottie quits his job and tries to overcome his fear of heights—without success. Then, later in the movie, an acquaintance uses Scottie's fear of heights to his advantage when he murders another character, knowing that Scottie will not be able to climb a tower at a critical moment.

OVERCOMING THE FEAR

Having a fear of heights is common and even healthy, since falling from even modest heights can hurt and result in real injury. The question, as with all phobias, is does the fear match the relative danger, and does the fear or even the anxiety interfere with a person's everyday life?

Anyone might experience a moment of dizzy concern looking out the closed window of a skyscraper, but this wouldn't necessarily be debilitating. Nor do we expect to feel this level of fear when faced with escalators, elevators, or a second-floor landing. But people with acrophobia can find even step stools daunting.

Fortunately, as with many phobias, there are techniques for managing the physical symptoms of the fear and, ideally, overcoming it. For a full description of these techniques, see "Overcoming the Fear" (page 199).

For instance, if someone is afraid to go down an escalator, they can practice relaxation techniques before stepping onto it. They can manage their fear by pausing for a moment, taking a few slow, deep breaths, slowing their heart rate, and releasing their tension.

A common—and often effective—treatment for many phobias is to gradually expose the person to what they fear. For those with acrophobia,

SAY IT AIN'T VERTIGO!

Vertigo is often used to describe a fear of heights, but that's not really correct. Vertigo is a medical condition, usually caused by inner-ear problems. People with vertigo feel that they or their surroundings are spinning, falling, or tilting. When vertigo is really bad, a person may become nauseated or vomit. So, while a person with a fear of heights might experience vertigo, you can suffer from vertigo without having acrophobia. Either way, you can probably cross "professional tightrope walker" off your list of career options.

this might mean first looking at photos that look down from a great height while practicing relaxation techniques. Then, in a steady, safe manner, they'd practice standing on a low step stool, then riding in a glass elevator, and finally standing on the roof of a tall building. They would move to each new step only when they'd successfully managed their symptoms at the previous one.

In a twist on that approach, some treatment centers now use virtual reality to simulate that feeling of being in a high place.

SCARE QUOTES

BARRY KRIPKE: "You're not afraid of heights, are you?"

SHELDON COOPER: "Fear of heights is irrational. Fear of falling, however, is prudent and evolutionary."
—From the TV show *The Big Bang Theory*

"Standing on the edge of a building, looking over the edge—it's so horrible. I hate it."
—Actor Tobey Maguire, who played Spider-Man in three films, on his fear of heights

AGORAPHOBIA

Agoraphobia (the term is from the Greek word *agora*, for "marketplace") is actually more complicated than a simple fear of public or open spaces. A person with agoraphobia is intensely afraid of having a panic attack in a place or situation where escape might be difficult or embarrassing. This is closely related to claustrophobia, or the fear of confined spaces, and many people who are afraid of wide-open spaces are also afraid of small, tight spaces. However, agoraphobia can be even more debilitating than claustrophobia: the idea of freaking out while on a train, in an elevator, or in a crowded room fills some people with so much dread that they simply refuse to leave home—whether for school, for work, or to see friends.

Agoraphobia is surprisingly common, considering how little we hear of it. According to the National Institutes of Mental Health, about 1.8 million Americans age eighteen and older (about 0.8 percent of US adults) have agoraphobia.

Agoraphobia usually develops as a result of experiencing a panic attack. A panic attack is what happens when, suddenly and out of the blue, we find ourselves scared stiff. Our hearts race, we break out in a cold sweat, and it often becomes quite difficult to breathe. We might think we're going crazy or that we might die. For no clear or obvious reason, our body's fight-or-flight response kicks in and we can't stop it, as though some predator really were roaring in our face and about to kill us. The symptoms of a panic attack so closely resemble those of a heart attack that sufferers are often rushed to the emergency room.

Doctors don't know what causes panic attacks, but they suspect that a combination of factors are involved. Panic disorders often run in the family. Stressful events, like a divorce or death in the family, drug and alcohol abuse, and even thinking patterns, may play a role in instigating them. And some evolutionary biologists even propose that agoraphobia is in part a holdover from our cave-dwelling days. After all, it's better to stay safe in our cave than to go outside and risk being attacked by a saber-toothed tiger!

However, panic attacks are such dreadful experiences that some people develop an ongoing fear of having another attack. They refuse to leave their houses, drive their cars, or go on dates, until agoraphobia affects all aspects of their lives.

FAMOUS PHOBICS

Interestingly, many people who suffer from agoraphobia are highly creative and have very active imaginations. If something could possibly go wrong in a public situation, they can imagine that it will happen to them. It is

PANIC ON THE GOLF COURSE

In 2012, twenty-eight-year-old pro golfer Charlie Beljan's throat tightened and his heart began pounding just before the beginning of the second round of a golf tournament. He feared he was having a heart attack. Somehow, he managed to make it through all eighteen holes of the course, at one point sitting down on the grass to catch his breath. At the end of the round, he left the course on a stretcher. He spent the night in a hospital, his spikes still on his feet. The verdict? Beljan's heart was fine. He had had a panic attack. The next day, he went back to win his first PGA tour event in the final round.

speculated that the famously reclusive poet Emily Dickinson was probably agoraphobic; in her later years, she rarely left her home in Amherst, Massachusetts. Sir Isaac Newton, aka the Father of Physics, seemed to struggle with agoraphobia for years following a terribly stressful time in his life.

The artist Edvard Munch may be one of the most well-known agoraphobics. He got the idea for his famous painting *The Scream* after a terrifying experience he had while out walking with friends. Indeed, this painting has become our cultural shorthand for this experience of out-of-control existential panic: In it, a figure with a skeletal, twisted head stands on a bridge under a yellow-orange sky, his mouth open in a silent scream as he clutches his terrified face with both hands. The painting has inspired countless pop-culture mash-ups, some serious and some silly—like the one featuring Squidward from *Spongebob Squarepants*. Even animated cephalopods feel angst.

OVERCOMING THE FEAR

Agoraphobia is one of the most crippling phobias. If it goes untreated, it can lead to depression and constant anxiety. People with agoraphobia often turn to drugs or alcohol to help cope with their feelings of fear, isolation, and loneliness.

Almost by the nature of the phobia, people with agoraphobia need help to overcome it. Therapists may prescribe antidepressant and antianxiety medications to help manage symptoms, and they work with patients to understand what triggers their panic attacks and find the best techniques for coping with the symptoms. They may accompany their patients to the places or situation that trigger the attacks to help them understand and confront specific fears. Therapists also often work with patients in their homes, since the phobia itself often keeps people venturing out to find, and continue to receive, help.

SCARE QUOTES

"I'm just from meeting, Susie, and as I sorely feared, my life was made a victim. I walked—I ran—I turned precarious corners—one moment I was not—then soared aloft like Phoenix, soon as the foe was by—and then anticipating an enemy again, my soiled and drooping plumage might have been seen emerging from just behind a fence, vainly endeavoring to fly once more from hence."

—Emily Dickinson, in a letter to her friend, describing a panic attack on her way to church

"I was out walking with two friends—the sun began to set—suddenly the sky turned blood red—I paused feeling exhausted and leaned on the fence—there was blood and tongues of fire above the blue-black fjord and the city—my friends walked on, and I stood there trembling with fear—and I sensed an endless scream passing through nature."

—Edvard Munch, describing the experience that prompted him to paint *The Scream*

AILUROPHOBIA

❝ Are you a cat person or a dog person?" People seem to love one or the other, with equal amounts of passion on either side. For many, it's a personality test: People who dislike cats say they find them to be sneaky, aloof, and neurotic. But even a dyed-in-the-wool dog person can't resist the cuteness of a tiny kitten. That's because they don't have ailurophobia. This genuine fear of cats is a centuries-old phobia that can reduce someone to tears, no matter how adorable the animal.

You might expect this fear to be called felinophobia, but the term comes from the Greek word *ailuros*, meaning "cat" or "the waving ones"—which refers, charmingly, to their waving tails. Some cat phobias can be traced to a childhood experience. Perhaps some-one, as a toddler, pulled on a cat's waving tail, and the hissing, yowling, scratching, freaked-out cat traumatized them. Many phobias start this way: A particularly bad memory gets lodged in the brain, and the person grows up with an irrational aversion to all similar situations.

Historically, ailurophobia often developed out of a medieval su-perstition or belief that cats are evil. In fact, in the Middle Ages in Europe, people became so convinced that cats were agents of the devil that they tortured and killed hundreds of thousands of them. Keeping or protecting cats was an offense punishable by death. As a result, the cat population dwindled to almost zero—and the numbers of rats soared. Consequently, rats spread the microbe that caused the Black Death, a plague that killed 30 to 60 percent of Europe's population. This wasn't the sole cause of the plague, but it certainly didn't help.

Even after Europeans realized that cats could help keep the plague at bay, many still remained convinced that cats—especially black cats—were witches' familiars or servants. The cats, they believed, roamed at night carrying out the witches' bidding, and sometimes witches even took on the shape of cats.

Out of that fear came some of the superstitions about cats that persist even today: that they can suck the breath out of a baby's mouth, or that it's bad luck if a black cat crosses your path. Indeed, these superstitions can sometimes lead to a full-blown cat phobia.

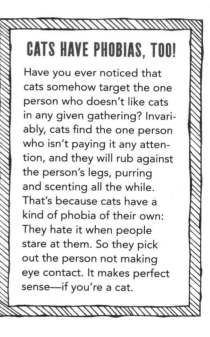

CATS HAVE PHOBIAS, TOO!

Have you ever noticed that cats somehow target the one person who doesn't like cats in any given gathering? Invariably, cats find the one person who isn't paying it any attention, and they will rub against the person's legs, purring and scenting all the while. That's because cats have a kind of phobia of their own: They hate it when people stare at them. So they pick out the person not making eye contact. It makes perfect sense—if you're a cat.

FAMOUS PHOBICS

Legend has it that one of the greatest military leaders in history, Napoleon Bonaparte, had a deathly fear of cats. Supposedly, an aide was passing the door of Napoleon's bedroom when he heard a great commotion. The aide burst into the room to find the general sweating and trembling and flailing at a tapestry with his sword. The problem? There was a cat hiding behind the tapestry—no doubt as frightened as Napoleon himself.

You probably won't find *American Idol* contestant Clay Aiken performing in any revival of the musical *Cats*. "There's nothing worse to me than a house cat," he told *Rolling Stone* magazine in 2003. "When I was about 16, I had a kitten and ran over it." He's been haunted by the spirit of that kitty ever since. Now, he says, they scare him to death.

OVERCOMING THE FEAR

Ailurophobia is one of the phobias that is often helped by familiarity with the thing that frightens you—in this case, cats. See "Overcoming the Fear" (page 199) for a complete description of how to do this. Start with gradual exposure, like watching cute cat videos on the internet. A person could then visit a friend with a cat or an animal shelter, until they feel comfortable enough to pet or hold a cat—that is, if the cat doesn't mind being held. Cats usually set the boundaries on their relationships!

SCARE QUOTES

"With my aversion to this cat, however, its partiality for myself seemed to increase. It followed my footsteps with a pertinacity, which it would be difficult to make the reader comprehend. Whenever I sat, it would crouch beneath my chair, or spring upon my knees, covering me with its loathsome caresses."
—Edgar Allen Poe, *The Black Cat*

"Some, that are mad if they behold a cat."
—William Shakespeare, *The Merchant of Venice*

AQUAPHOBIA

FEAR OF WATER

Fear of water is an ancient and fairly common phobia. At root, it is related to the fear of drowning, but not everyone is triggered in the same way. Some people are only afraid of entering deep water (even if they know how to swim), while others cannot bear to be near any body of water, no matter how shallow. In rare cases, the phobia can become so severe that people are afraid to take a bath or shower. This extreme fear merits its own phobia name, *ablutophobia*, and, needless to say, it can seriously affect someone's day-to-day life. The name *aquaphobia* comes from the Latin word *aqua*, meaning "water," "the sea," or "rain." It is also sometimes known as hydrophobia, which is a popular name for rabies.

Typically, aquaphobia is a learned phobia. Some kids develop the fear as a reaction to overly cautious parents (who may themselves have aquaphobia) who constantly warn them to stay away from the water. For some kids, their fear can be made worse by swimming lessons, ironically enough. A teacher who doesn't do a good job of helping small kids feel comfortable in the pool could help turn an understandable anxiety into a lifelong phobia. Also, aquaphobia might develop as a reaction to a truly life-threatening near-drowning experience.

FAMOUS PHOBICS

Actress Natalie Wood, who was known for her roles in movies such as *West Side Story* and *Rebel Without a Cause*, had a lifelong fear of water. According to her sister, Lana Wood, their mother had predicted that she would die by drowning in dark water. This frightened Natalie so much that she would not swim in her own Hollywood swimming pool.

Natalie's fear was tragically justified: In 1981, the then-forty-three-year-old actress drowned off Catalina Island. Although her death was ruled an accident, some, including her sister, believe that there was foul play involved.

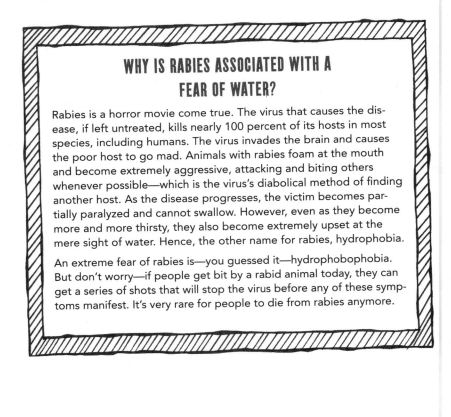

WHY IS RABIES ASSOCIATED WITH A FEAR OF WATER?

Rabies is a horror movie come true. The virus that causes the disease, if left untreated, kills nearly 100 percent of its hosts in most species, including humans. The virus invades the brain and causes the poor host to go mad. Animals with rabies foam at the mouth and become extremely aggressive, attacking and biting others whenever possible—which is the virus's diabolical method of finding another host. As the disease progresses, the victim becomes partially paralyzed and cannot swallow. However, even as they become more and more thirsty, they also become extremely upset at the mere sight of water. Hence, the other name for rabies, hydrophobia.

An extreme fear of rabies is—you guessed it—hydrophobophobia. But don't worry—if people get bit by a rabid animal today, they can get a series of shots that will stop the virus before any of these symptoms manifest. It's very rare for people to die from rabies anymore.

OVERCOMING THE FEAR

Typically, aquaphobia is treated through acclimatization. That is, swimming lessons. Building a person's confidence in water, and teaching them to swim, is one of the best ways to overcome aquaphobia, and many organizations offer lessons specifically aimed at aquaphobes.

SCARE QUOTES

"There is just one remedy, to throw the patient unawares into a water tank which he has not seen beforehand. If he cannot swim, let him sink under and drink, then lift him out; if he can swim, push him under at intervals so that he drinks his fill of water even against his will; for so his thirst and dread of water are removed at the same time."

—The ancient Roman physician Celsus, on how to treat aquaphobia

ARACHNOPHOBIA

Millions and millions of people can identify with Little Miss Muffet, who could not stand for a spider to sit down beside her. Arachnophobia—so named from the Greek word *aráchn,* meaning "spider"—is one of the most common fears. The real question is why, since most spiders are harmless to humans.

Some evolutionary psychologists believe that humans developed a fear of spiders as a survival mechanism. It would make sense—some spider bites can be deadly, so avoiding all spiders would have been prudent for our ancestors. We aren't, in fact, born with a fear of spiders, but psychologists have shown that babies and toddlers learn to fear them quickly—much more quickly than, say, butterflies.

Another theory is that a cultural fear of spiders developed in the Middle Ages, when Europeans thought that spiders carried disease and death during the plague. Of course, medieval Europeans got lots of things wrong about the plague: The real culprits were actually fleas carried by rats. Still, at that time, it was believed that if a spider fell into a bucket of water, the water would be poisoned.

ATTACK OF THE GIANT SPIDERS

Spiders—particularly giant ones—are favorite monsters for novelists and filmmakers. Not all fictional spiders are evil, of course. Charlotte, in E. B. White's beloved children's book *Charlotte's Web*, may have done more to endear spiders to people than all the nature documentaries ever made. However, Charlotte is the exception that proves the rule. Here are films that feature some of cinema's most notable horrible spiders:

Tarantula (1955): This old-fashioned monster movie is unintentionally hilarious. A huge spider pumped up on growth hormones escapes from the lab and terrorizes the neighborhood.

Arachnophobia (1990): In this horror-comedy, a South American killer spider hitches a ride to the United States in a casket and starts to breed and kill.

Eight Legged Freaks (2002): Another horror-comedy. A chemical spill in a rural mining town causes quite a growth spurt in hundreds of little, and then not-so-little, spiders.

Harry Potter and the Chamber of Secrets (2002): Character Ron Weasley's fear of spiders dates back to the time that his brothers, Fred and George, once transformed Ron's teddy bear into a giant spider. In this movie, Ron is forced to face his fear when he and Harry confront the giant spider Aragog.

The Lord of the Rings: The Return of the King (2003): J. R. R. Tolkien used the fear of spiders to great effect when he created the giant spider Shelob, an "evil thing in spider form." In his DVD commentary to the movie, director Peter Jackson said that he based his version of Shelob in the movie on the frightening tunnelweb spiders of New Zealand.

Not all cultures have a built-in fear of spiders. In Brazil, for example, children often keep spiders as pets, and Hindus in parts of India and Bangladesh release spiders at weddings to wish the couple good luck. Not surprisingly, there are far fewer arachnophobes in those cultures.

Scientists believe that spider phobias may be triggered not just by fear but by disgust as well. Like fear, disgust is a primitive emotion. It probably evolved to discourage our ancestors from eating spoiled food that would make them sick. Spiders and their webs are often found in "dirty" places like musty old basements or abandoned cabins—places that might make us sick.

Finally, spiders, with all those legs and eyes and hairy bodies, just look very strange to us. Psychologists have found that people tend to dislike angular shapes and dark colors, preferring light-colored, curved shapes instead. A spider's appearance, along with its unpredictable movements, can seem alien and disturbing. In other words, spiders seem built to freak us out.

FAMOUS PHOBICS

J. K. Rowling, the author of the Harry Potter series, has been afraid of spiders ever since she was a child. So she gave this fear to the character Ron Weasley, whose fear of spiders becomes a running joke in the Harry Potter books. In addition, Rupert Grint, the actor who played Ron Weasley in the movies, shares his character's extreme fear of spiders. Grint has said that the spider scene in *Harry Potter and the Chamber of Secrets*—when Ron and Harry must enter a den of spiders and face the giant spider Aragog—was easily the scariest he's ever filmed.

Other famous arachnophobes include tennis star Andre Agassi, singer/actor Justin Timberlake, and actor Johnny Depp.

OVERCOMING THE FEAR

Fear of spiders can range widely, from very minor and occasional to being too afraid to walk on the grass, enter

THE SPIDER ON EVERY DOLLAR BILL

Did you know that there is a spider on the one-dollar bill? Don't worry—it's not real. Plus, it's tiny. Look on the front of the bill, in the upper-right corner, at the shield shape that surrounds the number 1. A very small spider sits in a curve on the top left corner of the shield, as if admiring the web inside the shield shape. Some people claim it looks like an owl, but my money's on the spider.

your home, or travel if you think you might encounter a spider. Interestingly, and to make matters worse, studies have shown that people who are afraid of spiders actually see them as bigger than they actually are; the greater a person's fear, the larger the spider appears. Fortunately, arachnophobia responds well to the type of treatment called cognitive behavioral therapy.

For more on this therapy, see page 203. In essence, this therapy teaches us how to think differently about what we fear, and when practiced effectively, this actually changes the wiring in your brain. Before therapy, if you were shown a picture of a spider, the parts of the brain associated with the fear response would light up like a Christmas tree. After the therapy, those parts of your brain stay relatively quiet when faced with a spider. As one study put it, "Change the mind and you change the brain."

"After all, what's a life, anyway? We're born, we live a little while, we die. A spider's life can't help being something of a mess, with all this trapping and eating flies. By helping you, perhaps I was trying to lift my life up a trifle. Heaven knows anyone's life can stand a little of that."
—Charlotte, in *Charlotte's Web*, by E. B. White

The itsy bitsy spider crawled up the water spout.
Down came the rain, and washed the spider out.
Out came the sun, and dried up all the rain.
And the itsy bitsy spider went up the spout again.
—Children's nursery rhyme

ASTRAPHOBIA

FEAR OF THUNDERSTORMS

Astraphobia is one of those ancient fears that probably had our ancestors huddled under bear skins in their caves. It is normal to fear the destructive power of lightning or severe storms and to take steps to find a safe place. Fear of storms is common in children and pets (especially dogs). Scientists estimate that nearly 9 percent of people will have a storm phobia at some point in their lives, and there are several types. While the name *astraphobia* comes from the Greek word for "lightning," *astrape,* there is also brontophobia, or fear of thunder, and lilapsophobia, or fear of severe storms, such as tornadoes or hurricanes.

However, someone with astraphobia may refuse to leave the house if the weather forecast calls for even a chance of rain, and an actual storm will have them shaking and crying—even as they understand that there is little actual threat to their safety.

Perversely, the two types of people most drawn to watching the Weather Channel are storm buffs and those with astraphobia. Storm buffs enjoy watching a reporter standing by the ocean during a hurricane, but those with astraphobia are feeding their anxiety by constantly checking for weather updates.

AT THE MOVIES

Shakespeare, who knew a thing or two about creating powerful stories, set a powerful precedent for storms on the silver screen with his play *King Lear*, in which the king vainly rails against the forces of nature during an earth-shaking storm. Storms can serve as powerful metaphors for our vulnerability in the face of powers greater than our own, or to show how the human spirit can triumph over adversity. And sometimes—as in *The Wizard of Oz*—they transport you to a whole new world.

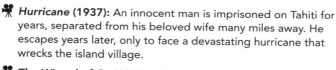

Hurricane **(1937):** An innocent man is imprisoned on Tahiti for years, separated from his beloved wife many miles away. He escapes years later, only to face a devastating hurricane that wrecks the island village.

The Wizard of Oz **(1938):** The tornado in this classic movie is probably the most famous twister ever. It's amazingly realistic, especially considering when it was made. The funnel cloud itself is actually a cone-shaped thirty-five-foot-long muslin sock, covered with a powdery brown dust. A yellow-black smoke made of sulfur and carbon completed the illusion. It must have smelled terrible!

Key Largo **(1948):** Most of the action in this classic, starring Humphrey Bogart, Lauren Bacall, and Edward G. Robinson, takes place in a hotel where the characters take shelter from a raging hurricane.

Twister **(1996):** Dr. Jo Harding (played by Helen Hunt) is a storm chaser. Her interest in tornadoes is personal: When she was a girl, she watched a tornado suck her father out of a storm cellar. As a result of his death, the girl developed a severe storm phobia but vowed to hunt down as many tornadoes as possible.

The Perfect Storm **(2000):** Based on a true story, this action drama tells the story of a fishing crew caught at sea during a killer storm.

While astraphobia can affect just about anyone, it is more common among people who have been affected by severe weather at some time in their lives. Kids seem to be especially traumatized by such severe storms. Of course, anyone who has witnessed firsthand the damage from a lightning strike or tornado knows just how dangerous some storms can be. Survivors of extreme storms

—such as Hurricane Sandy in 2012 or the devastating tornado that struck Moore, Oklahoma, in 2013—are at risk for developing post-traumatic stress disorder or other anxiety disorders.

OVERCOMING THE FEAR

Cognitive behavioral therapy (see page 203) is a common and effective treatment for most storm phobias, and therapists have begun using virtual reality programs to simulate storms as a way to lessen people's fears of them. However, since storms *can* be dangerous, it's also helpful to be prepared. Knowing you've done all you can do to prepare for a dangerous storm will help lessen worries.

STORMS ARE RUFF FOR DOGS, TOO

Does your dog hide under the bed at the first clap of thunder? Does he pace and drool, or cling to your side, when it begins to rain? Astraphobia in dogs, especially herding breeds like collies, is fairly common, and occasionally animals react in such extreme ways that it can be life-threatening for them. There are stories of terrified dogs that chew through walls and jump through windows in their panic.

Some astraphobic dogs begin to pace and whine just before a storm begins; veterinarians suspect that the sudden drop in air pressure or the buildup of static electricity bothers them. During a storm, they may be frightened by lightning flashes, or by the sounds of wind, thunder, and rain pounding down on the roof.

Your first reaction may be to try to console your fearful dog, but that just gives the dog the message that there really is something to be afraid of. Instead, give your dog a safe place, such as an open crate or a room away from windows, where the dog can't see or hear the storm. You might try distracting your dog with a treat or favorite toy. If your dog remains a basket case during storms, your vet can prescribe a sedative to help your pet calm down.

SCARE QUOTES

"Your chances of getting hit by lightning go up if you stand under a tree, shake your first at the sky, and say, 'Storms suck!'"
—Johnny Carson, longtime host of *The Tonight Show*

Blow, winds, and crack your cheeks! rage! blow!
You cataracts and hurricanoes, spout
Till you have drench'd our steeples, drown'd the cocks!
You sulphurous and thought-executing fires,
Vaunt-couriers to oak-cleaving thunderbolts,
Singe my white head! And thou, all-shaking thunder,
Smite flat the thick rotundity o' the world!
Crack nature's moulds, all germens spill at once,
That make ingrateful man!
—*King Lear*, Act 3, Scene 2

In the 1996 film *Twister*, storm chasers Jo, Bill, and Melissa are driving near two powerful tornadoes:

    JO (cow flies by in the storm): "Cow."
    MELISSA (on the phone): "I gotta go, Julia. We got cows."
    JO: "'Nother cow."
    BILL: "Actually, I think that was the same one."

"Better get under cover, Sylvester. There's a storm blowin' up—a whopper, to speak in the vernacular of the peasantry."
—Professor Marvel, in *The Wizard of Oz*

ATAXOPHOBIA

Ataxophobia—the term derives from the Greek word *ataxo*, meaning "without order"—is a fear of disorder, messiness, and untidiness. It's not just about being a neat freak, although neat freaks are more inclined to develop the phobia. For someone with ataxophobia, a messy room can spark a true anxiety attack—and they may find it unbearable to be in situations that involve disorder and mess, like finger painting, muddy baseball games, and food fights.

For many, the fear of disorder is actually rooted in a fear of losing control. Sure, we all need *some* control and structure in our lives; no one enjoys living in chaos. But an inability to tolerate the notion of *any* chaos or untidiness can lead to ataxophobia. Accompanying this is often a fear of uncleanliness; those with ataxophobia are easily disgusted. To them, a messy desk isn't just unruly, but gross and filled with all sorts of imaginary germs and creepy-crawlies. As a result, those with ataxophobia often compensate by cleaning constantly and planning everything so their world is orderly, predictable, and, well, neat.

Though it sounds similar, ataxophobia is different from obsessive-compulsive disorder (OCD), though having ataxophobia can lead someone to develop OCD. People with OCD are plagued by certain unwanted thoughts or fears—obsessions—that make them terribly anxious and usually lead to repetitive, compulsive behaviors or rituals. They might think, "Is my water glass really clean? Did I really lock the front door?" Then they must reclean their glass or recheck the door multiple times in a ritualistic way before their anxieties will subside.

Someone with ataxophobia may not develop compulsive habits, but obviously, obsessions with cleanliness and order are common to both, so they are frequently seen together. According to the National Institute of Mental Health, at any given time, about one in one hundred adults have some form of OCD. As with many phobias, the most effective treatment for ataxophobia is cognitive behavioral therapy.

FAMOUS PHOBICS

British soccer star David Beckham has admitted that he has obsessive-compulsive disorder and, along with it, ataxophobia. Everything in his closet must be arranged by color; he needs to know what he is going to wear the next morning before he goes to bed at night. Everything has to be in a straight line or in pairs. His wife, Victoria (aka Posh Spice), once told an interviewer, "If you open our fridge, it's all coordinated down either side. We've got three fridges—food in one, salad in another, and drinks in the third. In the drinks one, everything is symmetrical. If there's three cans, he'll throw one away because it has to be an even number."

David himself has said, "Walk into a hotel room and before I can get settled, I have to unpack, everything has to be perfect; the magazines the right way, the drawers in the right way, or whatever. It is, it's tiring. But it's more tiring if it's not done the right way."

The fictional TV show *Monk* is about a brilliant former police detective named Adrian Monk (played by Tony Shalhoub) who suffers from obsessive-compulsive disorder. Monk supposedly suffers from 312 phobias, including germs, needles, milk, snakes, mushrooms, heights, crowds, elevators—and, of course, disorder.

SCARE QUOTES

"A place for everything and everything in its place."
—Isabella Mary Beeton,
The Book of Household Management, 1861

"If a cluttered desk is a sign of a cluttered mind, of what, then, is an empty desk a sign?"
—Albert Einstein

"And this mess is so big
And so deep and so tall,
We cannot pick it up.
There is no way at all!"
—Dr. Seuss, *The Cat in the Hat*

AVIOPHOBIA

FEAR OF FLYING

A s with many phobias, aviophobia—the term is from the Latin word *avis*, meaning "bird"—is simply the most extreme expression of a fear or anxiety almost everyone has at some point. No one who has ever flown in an airplane hasn't wondered and worried about the complicated machinery they're riding in, the abilities of the strangers who maintain and fly it, and perhaps even the wisdom of hurtling through the clouds thirty thousand feet in the air in what amounts to an oversized tin can. Despite all the statistics that show that airplanes are perhaps the safest mode of modern transportation—one that's far safer than driving—it just seems safer to travel along the ground.

Fear of flying is one of those equal-opportunity phobias: There's a reason for almost everyone to feel afraid. Indeed, most people report having some anxieties about flying, and about 6.5 percent of Americans suffer from full-fledged aviophobia. The most obvious fear is a belief that flying is inherently unsafe. In fact, one-third to one-half of people who fear flying say that their main concern is that the plane might crash.

Some people hate the feeling of not being in control of their situation. Because many people don't have a very good understanding of what makes planes work, the idea of entrusting their lives to an airplane crew involves a genuine leap of faith. What—you mean we're supposed to trust pilots and maintenance crews we've never met, any one of whom might make a fatal error?

Others may feel trapped inside an aircraft cabin. Anyone who is susceptible to feelings of claustrophobia or agoraphobia knows that there is no leaving the plane after takeoff, and some may not want to risk having a panic attack. In addition, aviophobia might be sparked by a fear of heights, a fear of becoming airsick (or of being near someone who is), a fear of flying over or having to land in water, and so on. Sadly, the fear of terrorism is also among the list of reasons why people are afraid to fly.

FAMOUS PHOBICS

Basketball player Royce White was a first-round draft pick of the Houston Rockets in 2012, but as of the writing of this book, his future in the NBA is uncertain. The reason? He missed the beginning of his team's preseason training camp because, White admits, he suffers from anxiety disorder, which includes a severe fear of flying. Being able to fly to away games is a big part of being a professional basketball player—and not being able to do so might keep him from being able to play. White has gone public about the need for the NBA to address mental health issues.

He's Just Not That into You costars Jennifer Aniston and Ben Affleck have both suffered from aviophobia. Aniston developed a serious fear of flying after she was caught in an electrical storm on a flight from Toronto to New York City. The flight, which should have taken one hour, lasted two hours. She's gotten better, admitting to Jay Leno, "I'm not grabbing on the stranger next to me, like I've done." Ben Affleck's fear of flying started much earlier, as a nine-year-old child actor flying solo. His plane was hit by lightning, the engine caught on fire, and the pilot had to make an emergency landing. To make matters worse, he had watched a scary show the night before about child molesters. As they were making their emergency landing, a man sitting next to him said, "You know, if we land, they'll put us in a hotel. Don't worry—you can stay with me." The double threat of being in a plane crash *and* sitting next to a possible child molester is a classic recipe for developing a phobia.

OVERCOMING THE FEAR

In our far-flung, on-the-move world today, not being able to fly can present some serious obstacles: to career prospects, to seeing distant family and friends, to vacation choices, and even to romantic relationships.

The good news is that aviophobia can be managed and treated very effectively, and lots of programs and help are available. Occasionally, all some people need is a little education to get them off the ground. Learning about air-travel safety statistics, how planes are made, how they fly, and so on, is sometimes enough for people to manage any panicky feelings. After all, the greatest danger from turbulence is typically a spilled cup of coffee.

But for those with serious cases of aviophobia, facts alone won't do the trick. Traditionally, desensitization, relaxation, and cognitive behavioral therapy are used to manage symptoms and ideally get rid of the phobia itself (see page 203 for more on these techniques). There are a number of courses across the country aimed at fearful flyers. Some programs use the same kinds of flight simulators used by pilots in training.

Finally, some doctors may also prescribe medication, such as sedatives, to quell the anxiety during the flight itself. While antianxiety medications can be helpful, they have to be taken for a long time to be effective.

SCARE QUOTES

"I don't have a fear of flying; I have a fear of crashing."
—Actor Billy Bob Thornton, who has since overcome his aviophobia

"Both optimists and pessimists contribute to the society. The optimist invents the aeroplane, the pessimist the parachute."
—Playwright George Bernard Shaw

BOTANOPHOBIA

Plants may seem like a pretty odd thing to fear. After all, plants are everywhere—and they are generally considered benign and beneficial. But this is also part of what defines the character of a phobia—the fear is irrational, or unrelated to the actual danger, if there is any. In fact, botanophobia—which gets its name from the Greek word *botanikos*, meaning "of herbs"—sometimes occurs only in relation to specific types of plants or to plants in certain situations. For instance, one type of botanophobia is anthophobia, or fear of flowers. This may be because many plant phobias can be traced back to specific events in a person's life, particularly when they were young. The memory of a painful brush with poison ivy or stinging nettles, or the association of flowers with the death of a loved one, might well trigger a plant phobia.

Plant phobias can also develop in response to superstitions about plants. One superstition that lingers today is that plants must be removed from a hospital room or bedroom at night because plants will suck up the oxygen and harm patients. In short, this superstition is based on silly pseudoscience. As most people know, plants use photosynthesis to create and release oxygen. While it's true that at night (or once plants are in the dark) plants do respire, or draw in some oxygen from the air, they give off ten times more oxygen during the day!

An older superstition may actually have led to this idea. People once thought that fairies or evil spirits could hide inside flowers and might take possession of the patient as soon as it was dark—presumably because the sick were too weak to fend off the predatory spirits.

While plants might harbor microbes that could cause disease in some sick people, they don't pose any particular danger to people with healthy immune systems. Yet to some, plants seem dirty—after all, most of them grow in dirt. In a culture obsessed with cleanliness, it is not too much of a stretch to see why some people might therefore see plants as a kind of threat.

THE PLANT WHO ATE ME

We're all fascinated with people or things that don't follow the rules of the game as we know it. In the plant world, the prize for the biggest rule breaker goes to the family of carnivorous plants. Unlike most plants, they get some or most of their nutrients from insects or animals. Some species have been known to eat rats, so it's not too much of a stretch of the imagination to wonder if these bad boys of the plant world might just turn their sights to humans someday. Many of us have a tendency to attribute human characteristics to animals and even plants. The Venus flytrap, after all, gets its name from the goddess of love, who attracted men with her great beauty.

Novelists and filmmakers have seized upon this idea, creating some truly memorable plants that are fed up with being salad ingredients. The 1960 horror-comedy *Little Shop of Horrors*, remade in 1986, features a plant, named Audrey II, that craves human blood and flesh— and sings for her supper. Murderous mutated tomatoes try to take over the world in the 1978 camp classic *Attack of the Killer Tomatoes*. And carnivorous plants get *seriously* scary in the 2008 movie *The Ruins* (based on Scott Smith's book by the same title).

FAMOUS PHOBICS

Actress Christina Ricci told *Esquire* magazine in 2003 that she has a phobia about houseplants. "They are dirty," she said. "If I have to touch one, after already being repulsed by the fact that there is a plant indoors, then it just freaks me out."

One apparent urban legend (which is circulated widely on the internet) is that Sigmund Freud had a "morbid fear of ferns" and that he refused to eat them. However, it's doubtful that this was really true.

SCARE QUOTES

From *Little Shop of Horrors*:

SEYMOUR: "I don't know anybody who deserves to get chopped up and fed to a hungry plant!"

AUDREY II: "Mmmmmm, sure you do!" (Turns Seymour around to look out the window, where they see Audrey's boyfriend yelling and hitting her.)

CHIROPTOPHOBIA

I t's easy to see why bats have been traditionally feared by humans and why they are associated with so many superstitions and ominous legends. These nocturnal flying mammals hang upside down in dark places during the day. Then, after the sun goes down, they fly about using strange leathery wings and hunt for prey by listening to the echoes of their own eerie voices. They are creatures of the night, and humans have long associated darkness with evil, black magic, and madness.

For humans, strangeness and superstitions are ripe ground for developing phobias. Fear of bats gets its name from the animal's scientific classification—it belongs to the order *Chiroptera*—which in turn is derived from two Greek words: *cheir*, meaning "hand," and *pteron*, meaning "wing." Most bat species are not just harmless to humans but beneficial in general: More than two-thirds of the twelve hundred species of bats hunt insects, which helps to keep the populations of mosquitoes and other pests in check. Then, nearly one-third of the world's bats feed on the fruit or nectar of plants, making them critical pollinators.

People with chiroptophobia don't really care about how helpful bats are to the environment or our economy, however. What they typically fear is that bats will bite them—which can in fact result

53

in the transmission of rabies, a nasty viral disease that's spread by infected animals and, if left untreated, usually leads to death. (Rabies is often associated with a fear of water—for more, see "Aquaphobia," page 33—since symptoms include thirst and an inability to swallow.) In other words, dying of rabies is highly unpleasant, but it's also extremely rare. Prompt medical treatment is very effective at stopping the disease.

Even here, bats get a bad rap. Like any wild animal, bats *can* carry rabies, but less than 1 percent of bats actually carry the illness, and healthy bats don't normally come into contact with people. If you do see a bat though, definitely avoid it, just to be on the safe side.

However, if you want to know what really sealed the beneficial bat's reputation as a fearsome creature, you need look no further

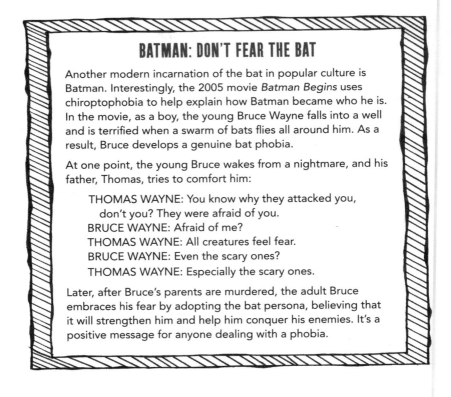

BATMAN: DON'T FEAR THE BAT

Another modern incarnation of the bat in popular culture is Batman. Interestingly, the 2005 movie *Batman Begins* uses chiroptophobia to help explain how Batman became who he is. In the movie, as a boy, the young Bruce Wayne falls into a well and is terrified when a swarm of bats flies all around him. As a result, Bruce develops a genuine bat phobia.

At one point, the young Bruce wakes from a nightmare, and his father, Thomas, tries to comfort him:

> THOMAS WAYNE: You know why they attacked you,
>   don't you? They were afraid of you.
> BRUCE WAYNE: Afraid of me?
> THOMAS WAYNE: All creatures feel fear.
> BRUCE WAYNE: Even the scary ones?
> THOMAS WAYNE: Especially the scary ones.

Later, after Bruce's parents are murdered, the adult Bruce embraces his fear by adopting the bat persona, believing that it will strengthen him and help him conquer his enemies. It's a positive message for anyone dealing with a phobia.

I VANT TO THIN YOUR BLOOD . . .

The final irony? Even vampire bats are proving useful to human society. Vampire bats have a special trick to keep the blood of their victims flowing freely as they drink: A protein in their saliva prevents the blood from clotting. Now, scientists are developing a drug from this protein that may help stroke victims. Most strokes are caused by blood clots that clog blood vessels in the brain, and it just so happens that the protein in vampire bat saliva is very effective at breaking up those clots, even hours after the stroke occurs. The name of the drug? Draculin.

than three bat species—located in Mexico and parts of Central America and South America—that are known to drink blood. They generally prefer cow's blood, but even so, it's admittedly pretty gross to think about, which may be why human culture can't stop thinking about it.

As in the case of cats, European medieval folklore associated bats with witches, as their familiars or even their alter egos. Witches were said to rub a few drops of blood onto their broomsticks, allowing them to fly in the dark without bumping into anything. Some believed that if a bat flew around a house three times, someone in that house would soon die.

Out of this, it was perhaps only a small step to imagine a creature that could transform itself at will into a bat and who lived on blood alone—that is, a vampire. Legends surrounding bloodthirsty vampires are centuries old, in Europe and elsewhere. Spanish explorers, steeped in vampire lore, promptly named the blood-drinking bats they found in Central and South America vampire bats.

Meanwhile, the locals they met, no slouches when it came to myth-making, had their own vampire legends. The ancient Mayans, for example, worshipped a vampire bat god called Camazotz, or "Death Bat," who killed dying men on their way to the center of the earth.

Then, in the 1890s, when Bram Stoker was researching for his novel *Dracula,* he came across a clipping in a New York newspaper about a vampire bat feeding off of a horse. This must have sparked his imagination, since he made Dracula able to shape-shift into the form of a bat (as well as a wolf and mist). With this, the quintessential vampire was created, and it has sunk its sharp little teeth into our collective imagination ever since.

SCARE QUOTES

Eye of newt, and toe of frog,
Wool of bat, and tongue of dog.
—William Shakespeare, *Macbeth*

Creepy-crawlies, vampire bats—phobia
I'm talking about phobia.
—From the song "Phobia," by the Kinks

CLAUSTROPHOBIA

FEAR OF CONFINED SPACES

C laustrophobia is very common. At least one in ten people admits to being mildly phobic about being in enclosed spaces, while 2 to 5 percent of the population has a severe case of claustrophobia. People with claustrophobia tend to have a fear either of being trapped in a confined space or of being suffocated; some get the double whammy, fearing both restriction *and* suffocation. Claustrophobia can affect many

MRI'S AND CLAUSTROPHOBIA

Medical research has introduced a nightmare scenario for those with claustrophobia: magnetic resonance imaging (MRI). MRIs are great diagnostic tools for seeing what's going on inside your body, but the patient has to slide into a coffin-sized tube and lie perfectly still for between thirty and ninety minutes. Plus, the machine is really noisy. As technicians have discovered, the combination is unpleasant enough to make almost anyone at least a *little* claustrophobic.

What to do if your doctor schedules you for an MRI and you fear a claustrophic response? Ask to be given a sedative, which is what many doctors recommend for getting through this.

aspects of everyday life. People may fear being inside shower stalls, tunnels, cars, or caves. Some with claustrophobia won't set foot on an airplane—not because they fear flying, but because they are terrified by the idea of being packed with others like so many sardines in a can. For some, tight clothing (like turtlenecks) or sleeping bags can set off those feelings of panic. Forget about getting on an ordinary elevator. "No thanks, I'll take the stairs" is the mantra of both the fitness buff and someone with claustrophobia.

The term *claustrophobia* derives from the Latin word *claustrum*, meaning "bolt" or "lock," and it appears to be one of those fears that we inherited from our ancestors, perhaps as a survival mechanism. Researchers believe this is based on an ancient fear of being trapped, with no possibility of escape. This may explain why claustrophobia seems related to its mirror phobia, agoraphobia (fear of open spaces; see page 26). If you lived in the Stone Age, you might feel equally threatened whether cornered in a small cave or exposed on a wide-open plain.

The fear of suffocation may be even more primal than the fear of being trapped. It's pure self-preservation. As it turns out, we

HOW TO CREATE CLAUSTROPHOBIA

In a famous 2010 news story, thirty-three Chilean miners were buried nearly a half mile underground, under some 800,000 tons of rock, when the San Jose mine they were working in collapsed. Specialists from NASA and drilling experts from several different countries worked together to devise a plan to free the trapped miners. It took nearly two months, but finally all thirty-three men were rescued from the collapsed mine—freed from what many thought would be their grave. The miners may not have been claustrophobic before their ordeal—few miners are, since it goes against the job description—but in the aftermath, many suffered from severe psychological trauma, including post-traumatic stress disorder. This is exactly the recipe for creating a debilitating phobia.

are hardwired to panic when we can't get enough oxygen. When oxygen levels in our air supply drop, carbon dioxide levels rise. Breathing in carbon dioxide increases the acid levels in our brain. Scientists have found that the amygdalae (where we experience fear in the brain) have a ton of specialized proteins that detect rising levels of acid, triggering our fear response.

This also explains why panic attacks can spiral out of control. When people have a panic attack, they often hyperventilate, which leads to less oxygen, more carbon dioxide, and more fear. On the flip side, this mechanism explains why slow, deep breaths can help us relax and calm down. Deep breathing increases oxygen, and so the fear response in our amygdalae subsides, in addition to simply relaxing the muscles.

FAMOUS PHOBICS

Actress Uma Thurman admits to being claustrophobic, which made filming the scene in which she is buried alive in a coffin in *Kill Bill: Vol. 2* a real challenge. "There was no acting required," she said. "Real screams available. It was horrific. You don't want to have that kind of experience." No, you do not.

In 2007, socialite and party girl Paris Hilton was released from a Los Angeles County prison to serve the rest of her sentence under house arrest because she was suffering from claustrophobia and anxiety attacks.

SCARE QUOTES

"When the cave door was unlocked, a sorrowful sight presented itself in the dim twilight of the place. Injun Joe lay stretched upon the ground, dead, with his face close to the crack of the door, as if his longing eyes had been fixed, to the latest moment, upon the light and the cheer of the free world outside."
—Mark Twain, *The Adventures of Tom Sawyer*

COULROPHOBIA

C lowns, with their goofy wigs, crazy makeup, and outlandish costumes, are supposed to make us laugh. Whether making balloon animals or pratfalling out of tiny cars, they are staples of circuses and children's birthday parties. But a surprising number of people, especially children, are terrified of clowns. In fact, when a British university conducted a poll to improve the decor of hospital pediatric wards, all 250 of the children they contacted said that they disliked the use of clown art in the rooms. Many found them scary.

The term *coulrophobia* derives from the Greek word *kolobatheron,* for "stilt." The ancient Greeks didn't have clowns like the funny figures we know today, but the word may have referred to "one who walks on stilts"—which is something that many clowns still do. Still, modern clowning goes back hundreds of years, to when royal courts had jesters who were permitted to mock and criticize the ruler. These clowns were trickster figures, an archetype common to many ancient mythologies. The mythic trickster—whether that's Anansi the Spider or Bugs Bunny, Coyote or Krusty the Clown—always breaks the rules and gets away with it. They upset tradition and don't conform to the norms of society. In myths, this unsettling behavior is often portrayed as ultimately good for society. That is, in their exaggerated wrongness, tricksters try to make us uncomfortable, so we might recognize our own foibles. By laughing at clowns, we are able to laugh at ourselves.

Which sounds fine in theory, until a real clown is getting in our business. Then, they may seem only threatening and not funny at all. Paul Salkovskis, an expert in anxiety disorders, told the BBC in 2008 that when things seem wrong or off-kilter, it unsettles people, especially children. Further, on a basic interpersonal level, we are accustomed to reading facial expressions to understand the feelings and attitudes of others. But the clown wears a mask, a cartoonish painted-on smile or frown that almost seems designed to hide his or her intentions. To enjoy a clown's performance takes trust: We must believe that, despite the clown's wild appearance and violent-seeming actions, he or she will never actually hurt us.

THE BRAVEST CLOWNS

Clowning is hard work. If you're a rodeo clown, it's downright dangerous. Rodeo clowns work in bull-riding competitions. Their job—aside from entertaining the crowd—is to distract the bull if the cowboy falls from or jumps off the animal. Some rodeo clowns prefer to be called bullfighters, since their job involves taunting a 2,500-pound beast with a bad attitude. Concussions, broken bones, cuts, and bruises are occupational hazards. Rodeo clowns must have a great deal of speed, agility, and courage, but there is one thing they should not have: taurophobia, or fear of bulls.

FAMOUS PHOBICS

Actor Johnny Depp has admitted a deep fear of clowns. He gets to the heart of the fear, saying, "I also have had an acute fear of clowns—a condition known as coulrophobia—ever since I had nightmares of them as a kid. I used to see their faces leering at me. I guess I am afraid of them because it's impossible—thanks to their painted-on smiles—to distinguish if they are happy or if they're about to bite your face off."

Rapper Sean P. "Diddy" Combs is also reported to suffer from coulrophobia, although he has repeatedly denied claims that he once demanded a "no clowns" clause in his contract. And Robert Pattinson, the actor most famous for playing a vampire, was so traumatized by watching a clown burn to death after his little car exploded at a circus, is now also deathly afraid of clowns. But not, apparently, of vampires.

Fear of clowns has risen dramatically in recent decades. In part, this may have been sparked by a real-life "Killer Clown," which became the nickname of the serial killer John Wayne Gacy after he was captured. From 1975 to 1978, Gacy tortured and killed thirty-three boys and young men in Chicago, Illinois. However, it was later learned that Gacy would also dress up as Pogo the Clown and perform, legitimately, at parties and charitable events.

Stephen King admits that he found clowns creepy as a child, and he created his own fictional killer clown in his 1986 horror novel *It*. The novel was made into a 1990 television movie, in which Pennywise, a monster disguised as a clown, lures children into the sewers and murders them.

Of course, virtually all real-life clowns are in fact good-hearted people. Most just want to make us laugh, and some do so in ways that serve a serious, even heroic purpose. For instance, the real-life doctor and clown Hunter Doherty "Patch" Adams, who was portrayed in the 1998 film *Patch Adams* by Robin Williams, has devoted his life to bringing medical care to underserved parts of the world.

OVERCOMING THE FEAR

Professional clowns take coulrophobia very seriously. Their livelihood is at stake, after all. In the United Kingdom, John Lawson's Circus has developed "clownseling" therapy designed to help people overcome their fear of clowns. The therapy is based on the common phobia treatment called systemic desensitization, which gradually exposes someone to a frightening stimulus in a nonthreatening way until it is no longer experienced as threatening. See page 200 for more on this.

In a 2010 interview with National Public Radio's Michele Norris, Paul Carpenter, a "clownselor" in John Lawson's Circus, said that anyone who wants to come in for clown therapy is invited to the big top before the circus begins. They meet the clowns in their everyday clothes, without makeup or wigs. Then, they join the performers in the circus ring, where they begin to transform into their clown personalities.

First, the performers put on their makeup, and then their costumes. Then, if "that goes well and they haven't run for the door," says Carpenter, the clowns try to get the people to clown around with them in the ring or even to dress up as clowns themselves. The idea is that when someone with coulrophobia sees real people they have come to know and trust transform into clowns, they will be less frightened.

SCARE QUOTES

"Want your boat, Georgie?" Pennywise asked. "I only repeat myself because you really do not seem that eager." He held it up, smiling. He was wearing a baggy silk suit with great big orange buttons. A bright tie, electric-blue, flopped down his front, and on his hands were big white gloves, like the kind Mickey Mouse and Donald Duck always wore.

"Yes, sure," George said, looking into the storm drain.

"And a balloon? I've got red and green and yellow and blue . . ."

"Do they float?"

"Float?" The clown's grin widened. "Oh yes indeed they do. They float! And there's cotton candy . . ."

George reached.

The clown seized his arm.

—A scene from Stephen King's novel It (1987)

"Can't sleep, clown will eat me . . ."

—Bart Simpson on The Simpsons (this quote inspired an Alice Cooper song with that title)

CYNOPHOBIA

FEAR OF DOGS

Cynophobia—the term is from the Greek word *kýōn*, meaning "dog"—is one of the most common animal phobias, especially among children. Considering the number of companion dogs in the world, cynophobia can be quite troublesome in everyday life, since avoiding dogs can get pretty tricky.

As with many animal phobias, cynophobia is often caused by a bad childhood experience with an animal. Whether it was something as innocent as being knocked over by an overenthusiastic puppy or as truly dangerous as actually being bitten by a dog, those initial feelings of fear can grow into a full-blown phobia; the fear of the trauma happening again can get transferred to all dogs. But a phobia isn't always a reaction to one specific incident. If you grew up next door to a home with a "Beware of the Dog" sign in the front window, and a growling, snapping animal in the yard, you might develop a phobia of all dogs. Or you might learn to be afraid because of well-intentioned but anxious parents, who always warned: "Don't you touch that dog. It will bite!"

Of course, some dogs are aggressive and do bite. Particularly with strange dogs, it's wise to approach them with caution (if not anxiety). This is part of what makes it easy sometimes for reasonable fears to slide into relatively unreasonable phobias: In certain situations and with certain animals, it makes good sense to be wary. Ideally, you don't want to be too afraid to visit your friend's house because she has a big friendly St. Bernard who wouldn't bite if you were wearing a bacon shirt. (I know; I had one of those dogs!) But if an unknown dog is straining at its leash or seems aggressive in any way, you aren't wrong to give that animal a wide berth, either. Though it doesn't change the situation, it's also worth remembering that, most of the time, an

WHO'S A GOOD DOG?

If you suffer from cynophobia, you probably wouldn't call dogs "man's best friend." But there are tons of reasons that these devoted, loving, smart animals are so adored. Want some fun-loving examples? Here are just a few:

- 🎥 *Beethoven* (1992): An adorable St. Bernard puppy named Beethoven grows up into 185 pounds of slobbering, disaster-prone fun! The first of many Beethoven movies.

- 🎥 *Homeward Bound* (1993): When a family leaves their pets Chance (a fun-loving pup), Shadow (a wise old dog), and Sassy (a cat who lives up to her name) with some friends while they go on vacation, the animals decide to go cross-country to search for their owners. Based on Sheila Burford's terrific book *The Incredible Journey*.

- 🎥 *My Dog Skip* (2000): This is a heartwarming tale (pardon the pun) about a boy and his dog growing up in Mississippi. Dog lovers, bring your hankies.

- 🎥 *Because of Winn-Dixie* (2005): When ten-year-old Opal moves to a small town in Florida with her father, she adopts a stray dog named after the grocery store where he was found. It's a sweet movie based on the novel of the same title by Kate DiCamillo.

- 🎥 *Marley and Me* (2008): John gets his new wife, Jenny, a Labrador retriever pup, which promptly flunks obedience school and turns their new home upside down. It's an engaging adaptation of the novel by the same title by John Grogan.

aggressive dog is the fault of the owner, who has either neglected the animal or taught it to fight or be mean.

Finally, because of the way this phobia usually develops, it is effectively remedied with the therapies described in "Overcoming the Fear" (page 199).

SCARE QUOTES

"Outside of a dog, a book is a man's best friend. Inside of a dog, it's too dark to read."
—Groucho Marx, *The Essential Groucho: Writings For, By, and About Groucho Marx*

"A dog reflects the family life. Whoever saw a frisky dog in a gloomy family, or a sad dog in a happy one? Snarling people have snarling dogs, dangerous people have dangerous ones."
—Arthur Conan Doyle, *The Case-Book of Sherlock Holmes*

"Dogs are great. Bad dogs, if you can really call them that, are perhaps the greatest of them all."
—John Grogan, *Marley and Me: Life and Love with the World's Worst Dog*

DENTOPHOBIA

FEAR OF DENTISTS

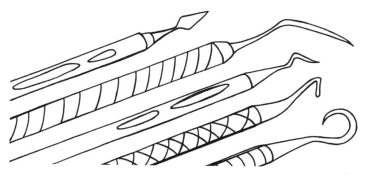

Very few people actually look forward to visiting the dentist. Even a routine cleaning can be uncomfortable. In fact, our dislike of dental procedures has become enshrined in our culture. What do people invariably say when they're faced with some horribly unpleasant activity or duty? "I'd rather have a root canal" or "I'd rather get my teeth pulled."

Fear of dentists—or, more accurately, fear of going to the dentist—is a very real and surprisingly complex problem. Up to 80 percent of adults in the United States admit to having some anxieties about going to the dentist; 5 to 6 percent are so anxious that they are unable to get the dental care they need. That's because a visit to the dentist—if someone with dentophobia even *makes* it to the dentist—is likely to result in the classic fight-or-flight symptoms: a pounding heart, sweaty palms, dizziness, trembling, and even chest pain and panic attacks.

There are nearly as many reasons people fear going to the dentist as there are teeth in the mouth. Indeed, dentophobia—the term is from the Latin word *dens*, meaning "tooth," and sometimes known as odontophobia—should not be confused with odonophobia, or the fear of teeth, which can also keep people from the dentist. However, the most common reason people develop dentophobia is the simplest: At some point, most likely early on, they had a classically rotten experience in a dental chair. Frequently, this involves physical pain. Perhaps they did not get enough anesthesia when having a cavity filled, or they have a lower-than-average pain threshold, or they had a dentist who was not especially careful or sensitive as they worked.

Pain in and of itself isn't always the cause, or the only one. Others report that visiting the dentist is emotionally frightening: After all, a masked person *is* wielding sharp objects and hovering over the patient's mouth. This can be a pretty intimidating and unnerving position to be in, which helps explain the tendency of most dentists to crack jokes or ask about your vacation—they're just trying to put their patients at ease. Then, some people are just plain embarrassed: They may have been humiliated at some point by insensitive remarks about their teeth, or they gagged on those awful X-ray tabs. There's nothing fun about possibly throwing up on the dentist.

In addition, dental phobia is unfortunately common in people with a history of abuse, especially sexual abuse. They fear being at the mercy of an authority figure, having to lie down for treatment, and having objects or the dentist's hand around the mouth and nose.

Finally, other phobias may also come into play: a fear of needles (trypanophobia, page 189), fear of X-rays (radiophobia, page 148), and fear of blood (hemophobia, page 85) may be enough to keep people out of the dentist's chair.

Given the fact that most people with dentophobia have actually had an unpleasant or painful experience in the dentist's chair, some psychologists believe that the disorder is actually closer to post-traumatic stress disorder (PTSD). By definition, phobias are fears that are excessive or unreasonable. In other words, the fears of many with dentophobia may be entirely justified.

FAMOUS PHOBICS

Abraham Lincoln was said to have had a great fear of dentists, and apparently for good reason. In 1841, Lincoln went to a dentist to have a tooth extracted. The dentist yanked out Lincoln's tooth—along with part of his jawbone (without the benefit of anesthesia)! Years later, in 1862, the president developed a severe toothache and consulted a dentist—reluctantly, one might imagine. Sure enough, the tooth had to go. As the dentist prepared to pull the tooth, Lincoln asked him to wait. According to one account, he "took a container of chloroform from his pocket, inhaled it deeply, and sleepily gave the signal for the dentist to proceed."

Of course, you don't have to go through this kind of ordeal to develop a fear of dentists. Actress and model Kelly Osbourne tweeted, "I have to go get my filling today and the fear is really, really kicking in. I need to get over this fear of the dentist but I can't!"

OVERCOMING THE FEAR

Dentists are well aware of the fact that many people are frightened of dental procedures, and they do their best to make the dental visit a positive one. If you are anxious, tell your dentist about it. Don't worry that the dentist will think you're a weirdo; he or she is used to patients with dental phobias. Your dentist will probably be glad you brought it up honestly, and they will be happy to work with you to come up with some coping strategies. You'll feel less vulnerable if you establish a good rapport with your dentist.

There are some common coping practices you can use to calm any anxiety while in the dentist's chair. Try counting or play mind games to distract yourself from what's going on inside your mouth. Imagine yourself far away, perhaps on a warm beach. Imagine that you are a superhero, and your superpower is that you are impervious to pain. Bring your MP3 player or listen to some music on your smartphone. Bring a squishy stress ball and hold it during the procedure. For more on relaxation techniques, see page 199.

If those techniques don't work for you, ask your dentist if you can use nitrous oxide (laughing gas) or, in severe cases, sedation. You can also seek out dental-fear clinics, which are becoming more common, where you can learn how to get over your anxiety.

SCARE QUOTES

"Some tortures are physical
And some are mental,
But the one that is both
Is dental."
—Ogden Nash

"Happiness is your dentist telling you it won't hurt and then having him catch his hand in the drill."
—Johnny Carson

"And so the dentist says, 'Rinse.' So you lean over, and you're lookin' at this miniature toilet bowl."
—Bill Cosby

DIDASKALEINOPHOBIA

FEAR OF SCHOOL

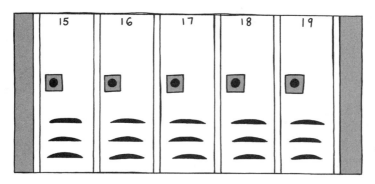

kipping school is a time-honored tradition. In *The Adventures of Tom Sawyer,* Mark Twain made playing hooky famous. But while Tom Sawyer was guilty of truancy, and of not liking school or his teachers, he did not suffer from a phobia. He had better things to do, and he felt he should be free to do them. Indeed, truant kids tend to be either bored or angry in school, not necessarily fearful or anxious about it. However, 2 to 5 percent of school-age children suffer from didaskaleinophobia—the term is a real mouthful that comes from the Greek word *didasko,* "to teach." If you prefer Latin, which Tom Sawyer did his best to avoid, then call it scholionophobia, from the Latin *scius,* for "knowing." For kids with this phobia, the idea of going to school absolutely terrifies them. Typically, school phobias most commonly occur around two periods: when kids are around five or six years of age and going to school for the first time, which can be scary, and then again at around ten to thirteen, when kids are entering middle school and adolescence at the same time, which requires no further explanation. In addition, moving to a new school can be a big trigger for a school phobia, which nowadays can be called school refusal. This is because a student may fear school for a specific reason (like bullying or an overall unsafe school environment), rather than from a phobia or anxiety.

FOUR CLASSIC HIGH SCHOOL MOVIES

High school is the ideal anxiety incubator. Students feel pressured to get good grades, fit in with their friends, and remain true to their own awesome selves. Feeling anxious about the pressure cooker you call school? Watch these movies.

- 🎥 *Rebel Without a Cause* (1955): James Dean plays Jim Stark, a rebellious teen who can't seem to stay out of trouble, in this film about adolescent angst. This classic movie, released less than one month after James Dean's fatal car crash, still resonates.

- 🎥 *To Sir, With Love* (1967): Unemployed engineer Mark Thackeray (played by Sidney Poitier), agreeing to teach a class of unruly teenagers in a rough London neighborhood school, tames them with real-life lessons and tough love.

- 🎥 *The Breakfast Club* (1985): Five teens with nothing in common must spend a Saturday detention together in their high school library. To the outside world, they were the Jock, the Brain, the Criminal, the Princess, and the Basket Case, but to each other they were the Breakfast Club. Quite possibly the best high school movie ever.

- 🎥 *Dead Poets Society* (1989): English teacher John Keating (played by Robin Williams) encourages his students at an elite boarding school to go against the status quo. "Captain, oh my captain!"

Children with a school phobia often complain about being sick in the morning before school. If they're allowed to stay home, their "symptoms" may miraculously disappear. For some, though, their anxieties create actual physical symptoms—headaches, stomachaches, nausea, or diarrhea—especially if they're forced to go to school. Younger children may throw tantrums; older kids often just refuse to leave the house.

For young children entering kindergarten or first grade, separation anxiety is the most common reason that phobias develop, especially if they haven't experienced preschool and are used to being with Mom or Dad all day. Older kids can also feel some separation anxiety, especially if there are problems at home, like abuse, divorce, or a death in the family. Staying at home gives children some sense of control, no matter how slight, over the situation.

OVERCOME SCHOOL FEARS—BEFORE THEY BECOME PHOBIAS

Students can have some very real reasons to fear school. According to the Bully Project (TheBullyProject.com) and the makers of the film *Bully*, 13 million kids in the United States are bullied each year. Three million of those students will be absent because they feel unsafe at school. Kids who are bullied and skip school don't necessarily have a school phobia. They avoid school because they don't want to get beat up, harassed, or treated like they carry the plague.

Some students have a well-founded fear that their parents will shame or punish them if they do poorly on a test, especially if they are feeling anxious about their college prospects. Others are plagued by performance anxiety when it comes to music auditions or trying out for sports teams, fearing that they will not live up to the expectations of others.

These fears are quite normal, but it is critical that students with school anxieties try to understand the source of their fears and, most important, to overcome them. Take the case of being bullied. If you allow the bully to intimidate you so much that you withdraw from social interactions or even begin cutting classes, then your fears can have long-term consequences even more serious than the bullying itself. Difficult as it may be, you should confide in a trusted adult—a teacher, counselor, or parent—to help you deal with the situation.

In the same vein, if your fear of taking tests causes such anxiety that you plead illness or skip class, you know that you'll eventually end up with a lower grade-point average—the very thing you wanted to avoid. You may have a learning disability that makes it difficult for you to take tests, even if you have the material down cold. Whatever the reason, school counselors can help you deal with your fear.

Education experts say that the more frequently students skip school or the longer they stay away from school because of their fears, the harder it becomes to overcome the fear. What began as a normal fear can lead to a true school phobia.

A school phobia may also be connected to extreme performance anxiety; teens in particular may fear failing, and so they resist school on exam days or when class presentations are due. The real issue may not be fear of school so much as a social anxiety disorder (for more information, see page 160). They fear being embarrassed or humiliated in front others, so they'd rather stay at home—and fail their classes—than risk acting or looking stupid.

People with generalized anxiety disorder are plagued by worries that something bad will happen. They worry about violence, tornadoes, or other disasters that could happen at school. In addition, depression, a learning disability, or a bad relationship with a teacher can all contribute to a school phobia.

As this makes clear, the reasons underlying a school phobia may be complex and interrelated. It's very important to figure out the causes, since an ongoing school phobia can have long-lasting consequences. It's been estimated that as many as 20 percent of students who do not graduate from high school suffer from some sort of anxiety disorder. If going to school makes you consistently anxious, or anxiety is keeping you from going to school, seek professional help or guidance from trusted adults.

SCARE QUOTES

"True terror is to wake up one morning and discover that your high school class is running the country."

—Kurt Vonnegut

"There is, on the whole, nothing on earth intended for innocent people so horrible as a school. To begin with, it is a prison. But it is in some respects more cruel than a prison. In a prison, for instance, you are not forced to read books written by the warders and the governor . . . and are therefore beaten or otherwise tormented if you cannot remember their utterly unmemorable contents."

—Irish playwright George Bernard Shaw, *Parents and Children*, 1918

ENTOMOPHOBIA

FEAR OF INSECTS

Grab your cans of Raid, entomophobes: Scientists estimate that, at any one time, there are nearly 10,000,000,000,000,000,000 (that's 10 quintillion!) insects in the world. Put another way, for every pound of humans there are about 200 pounds of insects.

It's rough to have an insect phobia. People with a severe fear of insects may find themselves constantly cleaning their homes and unable to open their windows or even leave their mostly bug-free home for the great outdoors. Note the word *mostly*. Insects are everywhere, whether you can see them or not. In fact, most people have microscopic mites (technically, not insects, but close enough) living in the roots of their eyelashes.

Let's face it: Insects are weird. In fact, they're downright alien. Many have hard shells, and some have hairs all over their bodies. Some have no eyes, and some too many. They also come with an abundance of legs, antennae, horns, segments, stingers, pincers, and wings! Worst of all, they are literally everywhere.

If this sounds like the ad copy for some sci-fi/horror movie, that shouldn't be surprising. Hollywood knows that just about

INSECTS IN FILM

Fear of insects is so ubiquitous in American culture that Hollywood often uses bugs when they want to get people screaming and squirming in their seats. There are two typical scenarios: either they make a tiny bug huge, so all its strangeness and threat is magnified, or humankind is threatened with destruction by "aliens" that are strangely, grotesquely insect-like. Both play on our fear that insects already rule the world.

However, there is a third scenario that captures a different existential squeamishness: humans who merge with bugs. Nothing could be scarier! Here are a few examples of each type:

Insects Attack:
Them! (1954)
Beginning of the End (1957)
Mothra (1961)
Empire of the Ants (1977)
The Swarm (1978)

Aliens Who Are Really Insects:
Alien (1979)
Starship Troopers (1997)
District 9 (2009)

When Humans and Insects Merge:
The Fly (1986)
Mimic (1997)

everyone is at least a little unnerved by insects, and, as a result, filmmakers have often dipped into that well to find inspiration for the next generation of perfect, scary "aliens."

The fear of insects is not at all uncommon, and it goes by many names. *Entomophobia* comes from the Greek word *entomos*, meaning "that which is cut in pieces or segmented"—aka, an insect. But this phobia is also known as acaraphobia or insectophobia. Fear of spiders, which are not insects, has its own name, arachnophobia (see page 36), and the fear of butterflies and moths, or lepidopterophobia, is surprisingly common. (Lepidopterophobics even have a website, IHateButterflies.com and an associated Facebook page.)

Entomophobes often fear that insects will spread disease. Insects are considered dirty and disgusting. Obviously, this can be very debilitating in everyday life. Yet most insects are harmless to humans, and all are beneficial in some way to the environment. Life wouldn't be possible without insects.

Humans do, however, have a good reason to fear some insects, as they can pose real danger. As described under ailurophobia (page 30), infected fleas carried and spread the Black Plague in medieval Europe, and it was only once people stopped killing cats, which could then kill the rats that carried the fleas, that the plague subsided. Today, mosquitoes are without a doubt the biggest worry; millions of people are killed each year by mosquito-borne diseases like malaria. The common housefly is also notorious for carrying and spreading disease-causing microbes. Naturally, it's a good idea to take commonsense precautions to protect yourself from these insects. Those with entomophobia, however, go overboard: Their anxieties extend to any situation or place where they might encounter insects, which is to say, everywhere.

Insect phobias also develop for reasons totally unrelated to anxiety over illness. Often, for no apparent reason at all. Those with a fear of flying insects, especially butterflies and moths, often report feeling freaked out by the constant fluttering of their wings. The fact that many flying insects travel in groups or swarms doesn't help matters, either.

IF YOU CAN'T BEAT 'EM, EAT 'EM

In many parts of the world, people don't fear bugs, they relish them. They happily chow down on fried grasshoppers, mealworms, caterpillars, and countless other insects. In fact, insects are an abundant and cheap source of protein and tasty, too. (I once tried *chapulines*, fried grasshoppers, in Mexico, and they were delicious!)

In the United States, most people are pretty squeamish about bugs in general, and particularly about eating them. What many don't realize is that the Food and Drug Administration actually allows a certain level of insect parts in processed foods. So, Americans eat bugs; they just don't realize it. In fact, a particular red dye made from smashed-up cochineal bugs is everywhere, from lipstick to ketchup. (If this freaks you out, steer clear of products with the words *carminic acid, carmine,* or *cochineal extract* on the ingredients label.)

Every year since 1984, the entomology department at the University of Illinois has sponsored the Insect Fear Film Festival, screening some of the best—and worst—of Hollywood's insect movies. At the concession stand, moviegoers can sample deep-fried wax worms, stir-fried silkworm pupae, and tequila-flavored lollipops with a worm inside.

FAMOUS PHOBICS

When actress Nicole Kidman was a child growing up in Australia, she developed lepidopterophobia, or a terrifying fear of butterflies. "I jump out of planes, I could be covered in cockroaches, I do all sorts of things, but I just don't like the feel of butterflies' bodies," she once said.

Woody Allen also fears insects, but that hardly counts, since the director-actor also fears elevators, tunnels, sunshine, dogs, children, heights, crowds, and deer.

It seems highly unlikely that the producers of *Fear Factor* could have persuaded either star to appear in one of their insect-themed challenges (or any challenge, for that matter), although their appearances would have been memorable. But the common aversion to insects makes the challenges involving cockroaches, slugs, and bees among the most popular with viewers, if not the participants. It's fun to watch someone else squirm while being asked to eat a live cockroach, because everyone gets the "ick" factor. Except, perhaps, the magician Teller (half of the duo Penn & Teller), who ate an entire cockroach—with apparent gusto—in one *Celebrity Fear Factor* episode.

SCARE QUOTES

"As Gregor Samsa awoke one morning from uneasy dreams he found himself transformed in his bed into a gigantic insect."
—Franz Kafka, *The Metamorphosis*

"Nothing seems to please a fly so much as to be taken for a currant, and if it can be baked in a cake and passed off on the unwary, it dies happy."
—Mark Twain, 1877

God in His wisdom made the fly
And then forgot to tell us why.
—Ogden Nash, "The Fly"

EQUINOPHOBIA

FEAR OF HORSES

Horses are beautiful, powerful animals, and many young people, especially girls, go through a horse-crazy period. Some of the best-loved kid's books and movies celebrate the wonderful relationship that can develop between children and horses, such as *The Black Stallion, Black Beauty, Misty of Chincoteague, National Velvet,* and more.

Nevertheless, it's also true that many horse phobias also begin in childhood with a negative experience of riding or falling off a horse. People report incidents of losing control of a horse, or of being bitten or kicked, and of vowing never to ride again. The power that is so attractive about horses can also be dangerous. There's a sad irony in the fact that a child's desire to ride and connect with a horse can be completely reversed if they have a bad encounter with an unruly, ill-tempered, or even clumsy horse.

This is the most common scenario for the development of horse phobias, but it's not the only one. Adults can also develop horse phobias, especially if they've been involved in an accident. No matter what your age, the size and power of horses can be intimidating. If you've ever witnessed an out-of-control horse, or even *imagined* what might happened if a carriage horse got spooked, you can understand how someone might develop a horse phobia.

Equinophobia comes from the Latin *equus*, meaning "horse," though it's also known as hippophobia—*hippo* is the prefix from the Greek word for "horse"; for instance, *hippopotamus* translates as "river horse." Thankfully, because of the way equinophobia usually develops, it is effectively treated with the relaxation, desensitization, and cognitive behavioral therapies described in

LITTLE HANS: IS FEAR OF HORSES REALLY ABOUT HORSES?

Perhaps the most famous equinophobe in history was Herbert Graf, or "Little Hans," as Sigmund Freud referred to him in a landmark paper. When Little Hans was four years old, he saw a carthorse that was pulling a heavy load collapse in the street. Afterward, he developed an intense fear of horses, fearing that one might bite him. His father, a big fan of Freud's, took him to see the doctor. Little Hans told Freud that the blinkers in front of the horses' eyes and the black around their mouths especially bothered him.

However, Freud didn't think Little Hans had equinophobia. He thought he was afraid of his father and exhibiting the classic Oedipus complex—named after the tragic Greek figure who unknowingly killed his father and married his mother. Little Hans, according to Freud, was in love with his mother and afraid his father would punish him for it. So Little Hans secretly wished that his father would fall down dead, just like the horse. The boy's fear of the blinkers and the black around the horses' mouths was supposed to be symbolic of his father's glasses and mustache.

In fact, Freud believed that most phobias were the result of these kinds of suppressed feelings, but psychiatrists today make a convincing argument that Freud's interpretation of the case was not accurate. In addition, while the object of a phobia can indeed represent some other displaced fear—such as a fear of death or fear of a parent—they are just as often exactly what they appear to be. Freud himself once reputedly said, to acknowledge the limits of his theories, that "a cigar is sometimes just a cigar." And, you might say, fear of a horse is often just fear of a horse.

"Overcoming the Fear" (page 199). Then again, this particular phobia isn't usually a serious hamper to everyday life, either, since it's rare to meet horses outside of horse-specific settings. That is, unless you have a sibling or child who is addicted to watching *My Little Pony* on TV!

FAMOUS PHOBICS

Kansas City Chiefs safety Eric Berry is fearless when it comes to facing his opponents on the football field, but he's deathly afraid of the team mascot, a horse called Warpaint. He won't run out of the tunnel until the horse has passed, and he retreats from the huddle if Warpaint and its rider are nearby. In a video that has gone viral, he can be heard telling his teammates, "Ah, hell nah, there goes that horse. . . . That horse. I gotta wait till that horse pass. I don't mess with horses, bro, straight up. He might come over and throw a tantrum." In an interview after the game, he told journalists that when he was a kid, a pony chased him while he was on a field trip. "I don't know if it was actually chasing me, but it came my way."

Actress Kristen Stewart had to overcome her intense fear of horses for her role in the 2012 film *Snow White and the Huntsman*. As a child, Stewart fell off a horse and was badly injured. "I hate 'em," she told *People*. But the role was worth it, and she got back in the saddle again.

SCARE QUOTES

"A horse is dangerous at both ends and uncomfortable in the middle."
—Ian Fleming

"A horse thinks of too many things to do which you do not expect. He is apt to bite you in the leg when you think he is half asleep. The horse has too many caprices, and he is too much given to initiative. He invents too many new ideas. No, I don't want anything to do with a horse."
—Mark Twain, 1900

GEPHYROPHOBIA

FEAR OF CROSSING BRIDGES

The fear of bridges, or gephyrophobia—the term is from the Greek word for "bridge," *gephura*—may actually be related to a fear of being trapped or a fear of heights. Almost by definition, bridges are precarious, unsettling places to be. Where the ground falls away, bridges continue across the void. Once on them, the only choice is to continue moving forward or to go back. Either way, you are suspended in the air and exposed to winds and the elements in a place where small mistakes have magnified consequences: If you lose control of the car or veer off the side, there is no shoulder to pull onto, no shallow ditch that will catch you. The idea of falling from a high, narrow bridge is terrifying for anyone.

For someone with gephyrophobia, crossing a bridge, or even thinking of it, can bring on a panic attack. If they are driving, they white-knuckle the steering wheel. Some are so afraid of bridges that they will drive long distances to avoid certain ones. Gephyrophobia often starts after some frightening incident involving a bridge. Sometimes, all this means is being on a particularly high bridge and looking down: You visualize yourself falling, much like Wile E. Coyote, but with sadly uncartoonish results. Others witness some frightening incident involving a bridge: Perhaps they saw one swaying in high winds, or they witnessed someone fall or jump from a bridge. It's not uncommon for phobias to develop and become more widespread in the wake of tragedies: This can happen with storms and horrible crimes, and it's been known to happen in the wake of bridge collapses (like the one that occurred in Minneapolis in 2007). The facts and statistics regarding the overall safety of bridges rarely alleviate the anxiety of someone with a phobia, particularly in the wake of a tragedy. Like airplanes, most bridges are very reliable and safe, but thoughts of a similar collapse can transform a low-level anxiety into a full-blown phobia.

In popular culture, bridges often signify some kind of change. They are literal and figurative transitions from one place to another. The change can be positive—bridges are popular places to propose marriage. But bridges are, unfortunately, notorious spots for suicides; the Golden Gate Bridge, in San Francisco, holds the unenviable record of being the top suicide spot in the world. In storytelling terms, crossing a bridge might indicate some internal change or transformation, while movies play on our fear of bridges by using the common plot device of the rickety or collapsing bridge (a good example is *Indiana Jones and the Temple of Doom*).

When people say, "We'll cross that bridge when we come to it," they're implying that there's a challenge ahead. And when you burn your bridges behind you, there's no going back.

BRIDGE DRIVERS TO THE RESCUE

In some places, those with gephyrophobia can request assistance driving across bridges. Every year, a service in Maryland drives about four thousand people over the Chesapeake Bay Bridge. About a thousand people request help in driving over Michigan's five-mile-long Mackinac Straits Bridge, a notoriously windy passage.

HEMOPHOBIA

FEAR OF BLOOD

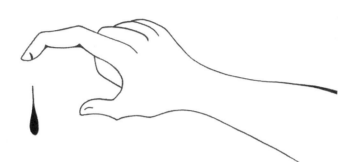

If the sight of blood makes you feel sick to your stomach, dizzy, or faint, you have plenty of company. Hemophobia—the term is derived from the Greek word for "blood," *haima*—is very common. Experts say that nearly 15 percent of us have passed out at the sight of blood at some point. And while many people with hemophobia don't report being afraid of blood itself, once they have this reaction, they fear they will faint again and make a spectacle of themselves.

With most phobias, the usual reaction to the thing that frightens us is the classic fight-or-flight response, which prepares you for some fast-paced activity: pounding heart, rising blood pressure, rapid breathing—the works. The response associated with hemophobia and other blood-injury phobias (like trypanophobia, page 189) is exactly the opposite: You pass out, or experience what might be called "playing possum."

When people with hemophobia see blood, their blood pressure drops, and they often lose consciousness. Scientists believe there might be an evolutionary explanation for this. Say you were fighting in a battle, saw blood, and fainted. Your enemies might think you were dead and pass you over. And if the blood happened to be your own, you would be less likely to bleed to death if you were lying quietly. This reaction might not win you any prizes for courage on the battlefield, but at least it would help you survive to pass on your genes.

Even if this is true and explains where the hemophobic reaction comes from, there's no longer any evolutionary advantage to it. The phlebotomist trying to take a blood sample won't confuse your fainting with death, and they aren't trying to hurt you. Blood phobia can prevent people from getting needed medical care because they fear blood tests, donating blood, or even helping someone else who has been injured. It has prevented many people from pursuing a career in the medical sciences.

OVERCOMING THE FEAR

Fortunately, there is a lot of help available for overcoming hemophobia and the "playing possum" reaction to the sight of blood. If you suffer from this, seek out a qualified therapist. One of the most effective techniques is called applied tension. It works like this: A therapist gradually shows you different pictures and videos of blood in everyday, nonthreatening situations (such as blood in a vial, videos of someone taking a blood sample or getting a blood test, and so on). When you begin to feel light-headed, you're instructed to tense the muscles in your arms, legs, and body for a few seconds; this helps raise your blood pressure so that you don't faint. Many people say that they can overcome their blood phobia after a few sessions.

FAMOUS PHOBICS

Actress Kristen Wiig apparently knew what she didn't want to be when she grew up. She once said, "I'd make a terrible surgeon. The fear of blood? Very high on my list."

Though she is a fictional character, Bella in Stephanie Meyer's Twilight books and movies suffers from hemophobia. She faints in biology class when they are doing blood typing. Oddly enough, this does not prevent her from falling in love with a vampire and then eventually becoming one herself. Presumably, all that exposure to blood cured her of her phobia.

SCARE QUOTES

"The 'Red Death' had long devastated the country. No pestilence had ever been so fatal, or so hideous. Blood was its Avatar and its seal—the redness and the horror of blood. There were sharp pains, and sudden dizziness, and then profuse bleeding at the pores, with dissolution."

—Edgar Allan Poe, *The Masque of the Red Death*

KAKORRAPHIAPHOBIA

FEAR OF FAILURE

It's safe to say that just about everyone has failed at some point in their lives, and as such, just about everyone has struggled with the fear of failure. Fear of failure is also extremely common among teenagers, who are trying so many things for the first time, and who may lack the confidence that experience brings. On some level, we all know that failing is possible whenever we attempt something, and we also know that occasional failure is inevitable, now matter how hard we try. But no one wants to fail. So the question is, how do you tell the difference between the expected anxiety that accompanies reaching for any goal you care about and a full-blown phobia? The answer is mainly in a person's response to the fear: Does the anxiety become so intense that it stops the person from attempting new things, or is anxiety itself the reason for failing? Then, if failure happens, what does the person do next? Do they hide and vow to never try again, or do they keep at it (and perhaps learn from any mistakes that were made)?

The Greek word *kakorrhaphia*—which means a clever or devious plot or plan—gives us the tongue-twister name kakorraphiaphobia. That Greek word, meanwhile, derives from *kakos*, for "bad" or "evil," which is also a root for the word *cacophony*. All of which pretty much captures what happens in our head: Fear of failure is a noisy, evil, devious plot that undermines our efforts.

For some people, fear of failure is closely linked with the fear of ridicule, which has its very own phobia name: catagelophobia. And it may accompany or be an expression of a broader social anxiety disorder (page 160), which involves fear of the judgment of others and being publicly embarrassed.

FAMOUS PHOBICS

Many famous people have overcome failure, and their inspirational stories show that failure itself isn't a true obstacle to success.

- After Michael Jordan was cut from his high school basketball team, he went home and cried in his bedroom. Then he practiced harder than ever, made the team the next year, and went on to become one of the greatest basketball players of all time.

- Oprah Winfrey was fired from her job as television reporter when she was twenty-two years old; she was deemed "unfit for TV." Oprah went on to dominate daytime TV for twenty-five years, formed her own network and magazine, and became one of the richest women in the United States.

- Albert Einstein was kicked out of school at the age of sixteen for failing several subjects.

- Director Steven Spielberg was rejected from film school—three times!

- In 1985, when Steve Jobs was thirty years old, he was fired from the company he started—Apple. Jobs returned to Apple in 1997, when the company was struggling, and he turned it into the powerhouse it is today.

OVERCOMING THE FEAR

There are many inspirational books and seminars aimed at helping people overcome their fear of failure and succeed at their goals. Much of this is excellent, and below I summarize some essential advice. However, don't be afraid to seek help, either from a therapist or a trusted friend. There may be other issues at work. But also, sometimes what we need most is someone who is on our side, who is actively supporting us and cheering us on so we don't give in to our fears.

Further, it's worth noting that people who suffer from kakorraphiaphobia are notorious procrastinators—which can guarantee the failure that they fear! They expect to fail, and so they don't put in the work necessary to succeed. Then, at the last minute, they throw something together and fulfill their own prophecy when what they've done is poorly received. If this describes you, changing your work and study habits is step one!

Here are five strategies for managing a fear of failure:

1. Remember that it's okay to fail. Success requires taking risks. When you take a risk, you've already succeeded simply by overcoming your fear of failing.

2. Worry and anxiety about what will happen are worse than actually failing. The consequences of failure are rarely as bad as we imagine.

3. Don't let a failure or mistake define you! Your effort and intention are within your control, whereas results are often not. Just because one effort failed doesn't make you a failure.

4. Practice, practice, practice. Don't get hung up on "talent" or "natural ability." If you put in the effort to develop a skill, you will be more likely to succeed, even if you don't achieve the original goal you aimed for.

5. Follow your passion. If you're aiming for something that you care deeply about, you're more likely to persist despite your fears.

SCARE QUOTES

"I have not failed. I've just found ten thousand ways that won't work."
—Thomas Edison

"One who fears failure limits his activities. Failure is the only opportunity to more intelligently begin again."
—Henry Ford

"I have missed more than nine thousand shots in my career. I have lost almost three hundred games. Twenty-six times I've been trusted to take the game-winning shot and missed. I've failed over and over and over again in my life. And that is why I succeed."
—Michael Jordan

"I didn't see it then, but it turned out that getting fired from Apple was the best thing that could have ever happened to me. The heaviness of being successful was replaced by the lightness of being a beginner again, less sure about everything. It freed me to enter one of the most creative periods of my life."
—Steve Jobs

"Do not be too timid and squeamish about your actions. All life is an experiment. The more experiments you make the better. What if they are a little coarse and you may get your coat soiled and torn? What if you do fail, and get fairly rolled in the dirt once or twice? Up again, you shall never be so afraid of a tumble."
—Ralph Waldo Emerson

KINEMORTOPHOBIA

Though it sounds like a joke, kinemortophobia is not a fake phobia. The fear of zombies—and especially, of being turned into a zombie—is very real, and on the surface, it's kind of a no-brainer (couldn't help it—sorry!). They're dead! They want to eat your brains! Thus, zombies tap into two powerful anxieties: the fear of death and one of our greatest taboos, cannibalism.

Perhaps this explains our culture's current fascination with zombies, which have lurched past vampires for the coveted spot of most popular monster; they may be fictional, but they're still a spine-chilling way of facing our collective fear of death. In any case, they're everywhere, from books (*Pride and Prejudice and Zombies*) to TV shows (*Walking Dead*) to movies (*Zombieland, World War Z,* and on and on) to roller coasters. That's right: Six Flags even has a new zombie-themed roller coaster, Apocalypse— The Last Stand. These days, what's a true kinemortophobe to do?

Surprisingly, the fear of zombies (the term *kinemortophobia* combines the Greek word for "motion," *kine,* with the Latin word for "death," *mort*) is far older than today's cultural fascination. It goes back many centuries and is tied to religious practices in

Africa and Haiti. For believers in these cultures, the fear is not of being *eaten* by a zombie; it's of *becoming* a zombie.

Today, the practice of creating zombies is most associated with Haiti's Vodou religion (which is today spelled *Voodoo* only in reference to sects in New Orleans); these beliefs and traditions originated in Africa and were brought by captured slaves. In truth, Vodou religion, as practiced by most believers, has nothing to do with zombies. This is a separate practice engaged in by sorcerers who diverge from the main religion. Whether these sorcerers have ever actually been successful in creating real-life zombies is a matter of ongoing debate. Perhaps obviously, this involves a secret, hidden world of ritual and witchcraft where what is real and what is imagined are deliberately obscured. In Haiti, zombies are the equivalent of ghosts in stories that some nevertheless say are true. Whether a sorcerer could turn people into zombies or not, he or she gains power so long as followers believe it *might* be possible.

Further, a zombie in these cultures does not match the current pop-culture version. In some descriptions, if a person dies an unnatural

ZOMBIE ANTS

There may be no such thing as human zombies, but there are bona fide "zombie ants"! There is a certain fungus (*Cordyceps*, for you scientific types) that shoots its spores onto unsuspecting ants. The fungus grows inside the ants and soon hijacks their poor brains. The zombified ants shamble out of their nest and up into a tree—just where the fungus wants them. The ants clamp their jaws onto a leaf—and die. Soon, a stalk sprouts from the head of each zombie ant. That stalk makes more spores, which then rain down on more unlucky ants below.

Recently, scientists have discovered that there's another fungus that actually preys on the zombie ant fungus. It prevents *Cordyceps* from spreading its spores—effectively castrating it.

Now, *there's* material for a horror movie!

death (by murder, say), their soul must linger in the grave until the gods give them permission to continue their journey. These souls may be snatched up by a sorcerer and locked in a bottle, and their undead body can then be used as slave labor. Thus, Haitian zombies don't eat living people; they're just pathetic, mindless creatures under a sorcerer's control.

In Haiti, new cases of zombification are reported each year, and they are treated like murders. This, indeed, would be enough to give any normal person a phobia about being made a target of a sorcerer!

One famous, or infamous, attempt to determine how sorcerers allegedly create zombies was made by scientist and ethnobotanist Wade Davis in the 1980s. He traveled to Haiti and, as he later described, found sorcerers who supposedly used a toxic powder to induce paralysis and mimic death in victims. These people were then buried alive in this state, unburied a few days later, given hallucinogenic drugs, and made to believe that they had become zombies and must do the sorcerer's bidding. The victims weren't really undead, but they came to believe they were.

Davis wrote about his findings in two books, *The Serpent and the Rainbow* and *Passage of Darkness*, but other scientists have since debunked his claims, and there is no definitive, accepted explanation for the phenomenon or any confirmation that it's even real.

SCARE QUOTES

"It is a truth universally acknowledged that a zombie in possession of brains must be in want of more brains."

—Seth Grahame-Smith, *Pride and Prejudice and Zombies*

MINDLESS ENTERTAINMENT? NOT NECESSARILY

If the idea of shambling, mindless creatures with a hunger that can never be satisfied sounds like a critique of modern consumer culture, it's no coincidence: That's just the point of some of the classic zombie movies.

- 🎥 *The Night of the Living Dead* (1968): Although zombies stumbled into the movies as early as 1920, this 1968 movie, directed by George A. Romero, is considered the granddaddy of all modern zombie movies. In essence, it created the flesh-eating zombie as we know it today.

- 🎥 *Dawn of the Dead* (1978): Many zombie-movie aficionados believe this 1978 sequel to *Night of the Living Dead* to be the best zombie movie ever. Plus, it takes place in a shopping mall. The zombie epidemic continues—and civilization has started to crumble.

- 🎥 *28 Days Later* (2002): Animal activists release chimps infected with a rage-producing virus, with disastrous results. Jim wakes up from a coma to find his city inhabited by zombie-like humans intent on his demise.

- 🎥 *Shaun of the Dead* (2004): This one is for those who prefer their zombie movies to be more funny than terrifying. This British comedy features Shaun, an aimless loser who decides to win back his ex-girlfriend. Unfortunately, there's a serious zombie invasion going on. It's not going to be easy.

- 🎥 *Zombieland* (2009): In this horror-comedy flick, zombies have taken over America! Shy college student Columbus (played by Jesse Eisenberg) hitches a ride with a zombie-hating tough guy and two sisters in an effort to get back to his family.

- 🎥 *World War Z* (2013): The world is plagued by a mysterious infection that turns entire human populations into mindless zombies. *World War Z* pits zombie against human. Based on the 2006 novel by the same name, which describes the social, political, religious, and environmental changes that resulted from the war.

KOUMPOUNOPHOBIA

FEAR OF BUTTONS

Koumpounophobia is rare, but it does exist. Some button haters—the lucky ones—cope by just avoiding clothing with buttons. This isn't that hard to do. Others, however, become uncomfortable if they're even around people who are wearing buttons. Obviously, this can make for some awkward social situations: "Um, I can't go to the prom. No, it's not you. It's the buttons on all those tuxedos . . ." People who are afraid of buttons may feel that they are dirty—their fears may be related to a general fear of germs (or mysophobia, page 104). Some people report that they are especially afraid of old buttons. Others are simply freaked out by the texture of buttons, especially plastic buttons, for some reason. As with many phobias, koumpounophobia may be linked to a traumatic childhood experience, perhaps related to choking on a button. One British bartender, whose aspirations of becoming an accountant were dashed by his intense fear of buttons, said that he was traumatized when a bucket of buttons fell on him at the age of two.

JOKE PHOBIAS

Some phobias are easier to understand than others: Fear of heights? Got it. Fear of snakes and sharks? Sure, that makes sense. But fear of buttons? Fear of dolls? Even pediophobics admit that their fear of dolls is a little bit bizarre. The truth is, with the right (or wrong) associations, any object or situation can seem threatening and become the focus of anxiety and fear.

Indeed, the strange nature of some fears has led to a whole new category of phobias: the joke phobia. Any extreme emotion or reaction is ripe for humor, and as the following mythical phobias attest, our fears can be funny.

➡ **Aibohphobia** (fear of palindromes): Take a close look at the name of the phobia and you'll get the joke. (Hint: A palindrome is a word that's spelled the same backward and forward.)

➡ **Anachrophobia** (fear of temporal displacement): This phobia is actually the title of a novel written by Jonathan Morris, based on the British science-fiction TV series *Dr. Who.*

➡ **Arachibutyrophobia** (fear of peanut butter sticking to the roof of your mouth): Cartoonist Charles Schulz made up this fear for his *Peanuts* comic strip.

➡ **Friendorphobia** (fear of being asked, "Who goes there, friend or foe?"): File this fear under "existentially traumatic wordplay."

➡ **Hippopotomonstrosesquipedaliophobia** (fear of long words): Well, this *may* be a real phobia of spelling bee contestants, for whom the name itself would give nightmares.

➡ **Keanuphobia** (fear of Keanu Reeves): This phobia is described by author Dean Koontz in his book *False Memory.*

➡ **Luposlipaphobia** (fear of being pursued by timber wolves around a kitchen table while wearing socks on a newly waxed floor): Another wonderfully ludicrous animal phobia courtesy of Gary Larson's *The Far Side* cartoon.

➡ **Zemmiphobia** (fear of great mole rats): Great mole rats don't exist (though normal-size mole rats do), and fear of them may or may not be a similar urban legend. It wouldn't be the strangest phobia . . .

FAMOUS PHOBICS

Apple CEO Steve Jobs was often called a koumpounophobe, but it's not clear whether he was actually afraid of buttons or just strongly disliked them. He was famous for wearing black turtlenecks (which are buttonless), but he also insisted that his product designers do away with buttons on handheld computer devices as much as possible. When he introduced the iPhone in 2007, for example, he did away with the built-in buttons that were standard on other smart phones, and he created a flat-screen phone with a virtual keyboard.

Further, the elevator in the Apple retail store in Tokyo famously has no buttons—it simply stops at every floor!

CORALINE

Author Neil Gaiman used koumpounophobia to chilling effect in his 2002 horror-fantasy novella *Coraline* (which was made into a wonderfully creepy animated movie in 2009). In the process, he may have done more than anybody in creating a whole new generation of koumpounophobics.

In the story, Coraline lives a perfectly ordinary life with her perfectly ordinary parents in an old house. Despite several warnings, Coraline opens a locked door and finds a passageway to another house. This house is just like her own, only everything seems better: better toys, tastier food, more attentive parents. However, the "Other Mother" and "Other Father" in this world have one significant difference—they have buttons for eyes. Further, eventually these other parents offer Coraline the chance to stay in this Other World forever, but only on one condition: if she allows them to sew buttons over her real eyes.

With this, Coraline realizes she's caught up in a real-life nightmare in which she must save herself, her parents, and three other children. Buttons never seemed so threatening, and no one has ever used fear of buttons so effectively.

SCARE QUOTES

"We made the buttons on the screen look so good you'll want to lick them."
—Steve Jobs

"How big are souls anyway?" asked Coraline.

The other mother sat down at the kitchen table and leaned back against the wall, saying nothing. She picked at her teeth with a long crimson-varnished fingernail, then she tapped the finger, gently, tap-tap-tap against the polished black surface of her black button eyes.

—Neil Gaiman, *Coraline*

MUSOPHOBIA

FEAR OF MICE OR RATS

Musophobia is one of the most common animal phobias. Of course, many people think mice are cute, and others keep the intelligent rat as a pet. Not everyone fears these rodents. But see an unexpected mouse scurrying across the kitchen floor, and you may well race from the room or find yourself standing on a chair and screaming. Few people find it adorable to see any rodent feasting on our food or scurrying over our garbage. Typically, these sorts of encounters elicit strong negative feelings, which for some can develop into true musophobia (the term comes from the Latin word for "mouse," *mus*). Some also call this *suriphobia*, derived from "mouse" in French, *souris*.

A PATRON SAINT FOR MUSOPHOBES

Who knew? Gertrude of Nivelles (in present-day Belgium), a seventh-century abbess, is the patron saint of musophobes. That is, she is invoked to protect against rats, and she is often depicted as a woman with mice either at her feet or running up her cloak or her staff. Ironically, she is also the patron saint of cats, and she is also often shown with a cat nearby.

MICE AND RATS IN POPULAR CULTURE: FRIEND AND FOE

If you can get beyond the fact that rats and mice have been responsible for spreading disease and nibbling on our food, you have to acknowledge that they can be pretty darn cute, what with their twitchy little whiskers and their shiny eyes. Mice, especially, have a certain charming vulnerability that makes for loveable characters in books and movies.

 ***Steamboat Willie* (1928):** The eight-minute movie that launched the career of the most famous mouse of all time, Mickey Mouse.

🎥 ***Stuart Little* (1945):** E. B. White's classic book about a mouse born to a family of humans, was made into a live-action and computer-animation movie in 1999. The movie has its moments, but White's writing brings the debonair little chap to life better than any special effects in the movie.

🎥 ***An American Tail* (1986):** Fievel, a young Russian mouse, is separated from his parents on the way to America, a land with no cats. Boy, were they surprised. It's cute and has some great music, especially "Somewhere Out There."

Rats, on the other hand, are another matter. Cute? Not so much, especially if you're used to the New York subway type. Rats in pop culture tend to have a certain sly cunning, even if they're good guys at heart. And when they're bad guys, they can be very bad indeed. Why do you think we call them rats? Tough-guy actor Jimmy Cagney's famous line "Come out and take it, you dirty, yellow-bellied rat, or I'll give it to you through the door!" from the 1932 movie *Taxi!* just wouldn't have had the same kick if he'd called his opponent a mouse.

 ***Charlotte's Web* (1952):** E. B. White comes through with yet another memorable rodent character in this book, which was made into a movie in 1973 and again in 2006. Who can forget Templeton the gluttonous rat?

🎥 ***Willard* (1971)** and ***Ben* (1972):** For pure rat evil, you should watch these movies. Check out the performance of the theme song to *Ben* by a young Michael Jackson and try not to feel shivers run down your spine.

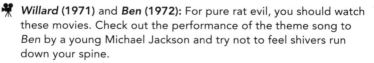 ***Ratatouille* (2007):** Against all odds, a French rat named Remy dreams of becoming a great chef. He may be one of the most loveable movie rats ever, but he's got a certain ratlike swagger. "You're in Paris now, baby! My town! No brother of mine eats rejectamenta in my town!"

Clearly, many people fear rats and mice because their presence is a signal of uncleanliness. They ruin our food by eating it, and many believe that the rodents are themselves inherently dirty. Also, rodents are historically notorious for carrying and spreading deadly diseases. In the Middle Ages, rats were the primary carriers of the bubonic plague—a disease that killed at least one-third of the Europe's population over the course of a succession of outbreaks over several hundred years. This was certainly enough to instill a worldwide cultural fear of rats.

Fortunately, with the advent of modern medicine, the plague is no longer the danger it once was. Further, though wild mice and rats do still spread other diseases, these generally don't threaten people.

Still, squeamishness regarding rats and mice is widespread, and if you find you avoid all situations in which they might be encountered (even those "cute" mice kept as pets), know that you are far from alone.

FAMOUS PHOBICS

It's only an urban legend that Walt Disney, who launched his empire with an adorable cartoon character named Mickey Mouse, was a musophobe. If only it were true! Disney was actually very fond of mice. When he was a young artist at the Laugh-O-Gram Studio in Kansas City, he used to rescue them from his office wastebasket in the mornings. He kept several in a cage on his drawing board and liked to watch their antics. One of the mice, which he named Mortimer, became quite tame, and he got the idea of creating a series of cartoons based on his little friend. The rest, as they say, is history.

And is it really true that elephants are afraid of mice? Nope. That myth dates all the way back to the first century AD, when Pliny the Elder wrote, "Of all living Creatures [elephants] most detest a Mouse; and if they perceive that their Provender lying in the Manger hath been touched by it, they will not touch it." It's not clear where Pliny got this idea, but he was also the genius who brought us the notion that porcupines shoot their quills.

SCARE QUOTES

"For many hours the immediate vicinity of the low framework upon which I lay had been literally swarming with rats. They were wild, bold, ravenous; their red eyes glaring upon me as if they waited but for motionlessness on my part to make me their prey. 'To what food,' I thought, 'have they been accustomed in the well?'"
—Edgar Allen Poe, *The Pit and the Pendulum*

"I love Mickey Mouse more than any woman I have ever known."
—Walt Disney

MYSOPHOBIA

FEAR OF GERMS

Mysophobia is another one of those phobias that is based on a good impulse—since avoiding germs is important for avoiding sickness—but which takes the impulse way too far. Everyone knows that you should wash your hands after going to the bathroom, and after sneezing into your hands, and as a general precaution before preparing or handling food. And there's nothing wrong with keeping a bottle of hand sanitizer in your bag or purse for a quick cleanse in places where soap and water aren't available. Good hygiene is a prudent way to maintain good health.

So how can you tell when a healthy fear of germs, dirt, and contamination is becoming an unhealthy anxiety and perhaps a full-blown case of mysophobia (the term comes from the Greek word *musus*, meaning "uncleanliness")? Consider to what degree your fear of germs impacts your life and relationships. People with a true germ phobia are so afraid of microbes that they go to extraordinary lengths to prevent contamination of any sort. They often wash their hands obsessively. They may avoid using public bathrooms, crowded rooms, shaking hands, touching an animal, or sharing a sip of soda—anything that they think might expose them to germs. Some can't even bring themselves to kiss the people they love! Then, if they do become exposed to germs, they may experience all of the classic symptoms of an anxiety attack: breathlessness, nausea, a pounding heart, and a feeling that they must escape.

In fact, people with mysophobia may appear to mirror the symptoms of someone with obsessive-compulsive disorder (OCD). For instance, both groups wash their hands a lot—way too much. (This is actually counterproductive for someone with mysophobia, as excessive handwashing dries the skin, which cracks and make it more prone to infection.) However, while mysophobia may lead to OCD, they're not the same disorder. People with

GERMS AREN'T ALL BAD!

Those with mysophobia might want to stop reading right now. The truth is, our bodies are actually teeming with bacteria, from head to toe, inside and out. There are ten times more bacterial cells in our bodies than human cells—and that's a good thing because they keep us healthy. They make vitamins, help digest food, keep our immune systems healthy, and crowd out disease-causing bacteria.

Many scientists and public health professionals believe that our obsession with cleanliness is actually making us sicker. There is quite a bit of evidence to suggest that little kids need to be exposed to germs so that their immune systems can develop properly. In our super-clean world, the cells of developing immune systems just aren't busy enough fighting off infections. According to the hygiene hypothesis, our immune cells begin to mount allergic reactions instead, which explains the rise in asthma and allergies, and perhaps even autism.

What's more, the overuse of antibacterial products and antibiotics actually selects for bacteria that survive these compounds. This is the unintended consequence of our war on germs: We are steadily creating superbugs that are resistant to our antibacterial weapons. The moral of the story? A little dirt never hurt anyone.

OCD wash their hands repeatedly and ritualistically because they feel compelled to do so (for more on this, see ataxophobia, page 44). For them, handwashing has nothing to do with getting clean, while someone with mysophobia washes over and over specifically to get rid of germs.

Mysophobia can arise as an exaggerated response to our culture-wide fear of germs. Someone may first learn this anxiety from overprotective parents who constantly worry about germs and infections, and this fear then gets amplified by an American culture that is seemingly obsessed with killing germs. Today, people seem to have the notion that good old soap and water are not enough, and the bacteria-killing strength of household cleaners, sponges, wipes, hand sanitizers, body soaps, clothing, and even lip gloss is constantly advertised. Other countries and cultures have very different attitudes toward germs and personal hygiene, so how did this occur in the United States?

Katherine Ashenburg, the author of *The Dirt on Clean: An Unsanitized History,* says that our obsession with cleanliness began after the Civil War. Health professionals found that they could prevent a lot of people from dying just by keeping them clean. Imagine that! Then, in typical American fashion, we apparently decided that if a little cleanliness were a good thing, a lot would be phenomenal. We have since become convinced that getting rid of all germs is the key to health, and companies and advertisers are only too happy to sell us products to keep our bodies and environment as germ-free as possible. However, this attitude is mistaken, for bacteria are not only ubiquitous but often beneficial (see "Germs Aren't All Bad!" page 105).

FAMOUS PHOBICS

Perhaps the world's most famous mysophobe was Howard Hughes, an American aviator, businessman, investor, and filmmaker who was one of the wealthiest men alive when he died in 1976 at the age of seventy.

Toward the end of his life, Hughes insisted on lying naked in bed in a darkened room he thought to be germ-free. He wore tissue boxes on his feet to protect them, and he burned his clothing if someone near him became sick. He gave his staff elaborate instructions on preparing his food, and he insisted that they wash their hands several times and layer their hands with paper towels when serving him. Ironically, he rarely bathed or brushed his teeth; he was convinced that the only germs that could harm him came from outside.

Researchers believe that Hughes learned his fear of germs from his mother. She was terrified that he would catch polio, a major health threat when he was a boy, and checked him every day for disease.

SCARE QUOTES

"Personally, I never take any special precautions against germs. I don't shy away from people who sneeze and cough, I don't wipe off the telephone, I don't cover the toilet seat, and if I drop food on the floor, I pick it up and eat it. . . . I never get infections . . . and you know why? Because I have a good, strong immune system, and it gets lots of practice."
—Comedian George Carlin

NEOPHOBIA

FEAR OF NEW THINGS OR EXPERIENCES

F ear of change is common: We fear that we'll fail if we try something new. We fear that we'll look stupid if we take a risk. We fear making decisions that we may come to regret. We even fear stepping out of our basic comfort zones. It sometimes seems easier to stay with what you know than to try something (or someone) new. People who fear making decisions often cope with the problem by procrastinating ("I'll sleep on it—another night . . ."). Of course, this tends to cause problems of its own. If we feel that we are stuck in a rut, most of us are able to take a deep breath, muster our courage, and try something new. But if the fear prevents you from moving ahead with your life—if, for example, you are involved in an unhappy relationship but you just can't find the will to leave—you may have a phobia. (Assuming, of course, that you are not in an abusive relationship where you fear that you might be physically harmed if you leave.)

Children are often suspicious of change; researchers even have a name for that phase that many notoriously picky eaters go through: food neophobia. Evolutionary biologists suggest that it's a survival tactic. If you're old enough to forage for your own food, but inexperienced enough to know what might kill you, it's best to play it safe. There is also likely to be a genetic reason why little Johnny will only eat macaroni and cheese: Many people are born with an inherited heightened taste response. They're called supertasters. To them, vegetables like broccoli are unpleasantly bitter. Most children, even supertasters, eventually outgrow their food neophobia.

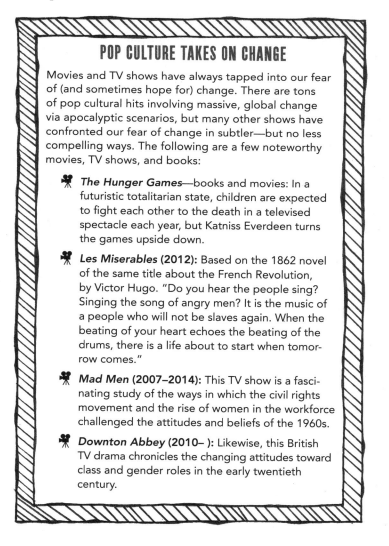

POP CULTURE TAKES ON CHANGE

Movies and TV shows have always tapped into our fear of (and sometimes hope for) change. There are tons of pop cultural hits involving massive, global change via apocalyptic scenarios, but many other shows have confronted our fear of change in subtler—but no less compelling ways. The following are a few noteworthy movies, TV shows, and books:

- *The Hunger Games*—books and movies: In a futuristic totalitarian state, children are expected to fight each other to the death in a televised spectacle each year, but Katniss Everdeen turns the games upside down.

- *Les Miserables* (2012): Based on the 1862 novel of the same title about the French Revolution, by Victor Hugo. "Do you hear the people sing? Singing the song of angry men? It is the music of a people who will not be slaves again. When the beating of your heart echoes the beating of the drums, there is a life about to start when tomorrow comes."

- *Mad Men* (2007–2014): This TV show is a fascinating study of the ways in which the civil rights movement and the rise of women in the workforce challenged the attitudes and beliefs of the 1960s.

- *Downton Abbey* (2010–): Likewise, this British TV drama chronicles the changing attitudes toward class and gender roles in the early twentieth century.

Neophobia may be triggered by specific events, but there is a growing body of evidence to indicate that people with certain personalities are more prone to fear change. People with outgoing, Type A personalities love change—they are always looking for a better way of doing things, and they don't mind taking risks. Detail-oriented type C personalities have less tolerance for risk; they are much more cautious about making changes.

Neophobia—or at any rate, a dislike of change—can operate on a societal level, too. The terms *left* and *right* first appeared during the French Revolution, when members of the national assembly divided into supporters of the king on the right and supporters of the revolution on the left.

Recent studies have shown that people who consider themselves liberal or conservative don't just vote differently, they think differently. Conservatives, for example, tend to be less open to new experiences than liberals. While they tend to be more anxious, they are also better at assessing potential threats than liberals. This is not to say that conservatives are neophobic, or that liberals are crazy risk takers, but there is a definite difference in the way the two groups think about new ideas and experiences. We've seen a huge cultural shift in the past few years about a variety of things—marriage for same-sex couples and religious tolerance (or intolerance), to name a couple of hot-topic issues. The result is that we're seeing an ever-increasing rift between those who want to maintain the status quo and those who want to change it.

SCARE QUOTES

"All changes, even the most longed for, have their melancholy; for what we leaved behind us is a part of ourselves; we must die to one life before we can enter another."
—Anatole France

"Progress is a nice word. But change is its motivator. And change has its enemies."
—Robert Kennedy

"Our dilemma is that we hate change and love it at the same time; what we really want is for things to remain the same but get better."
—Sydney J. Harris

"*Plus ça change, plus c'est la meme chose.*" (Loosely translated, "The more things change, the more they stay the same."
—Jean-Baptiste Alphonse Karr

"If you fear change, leave it here."
—Tip bar sign

"Here's to the crazy ones. The misfits. The rebels. The trouble-makers. The round pegs in the square holes. The ones who see things differently. They're not fond of rules. And they have no respect for the status quo. You can quote them, disagree with them, glorify or vilify them. About the only thing you can't do is ignore them. Because they change things. They push the human race forward. And while some may see them as the crazy ones, we see genius. Because the people who are crazy enough to think they can change the world, are the ones who do."
—The text for Apple's "Crazy Ones" TV commercials, for their Think Different campaign

NOMOPHOBIA

T he newest phobia on the market today may be nomophobia, aka cell-phone addiction, as characterized by certain British researchers. *Nomo* is short for "no mobile," and nomophobia describes the feelings of severe anxiety that ensue when people can't find their cell phone, when their cell-phone battery or credit runs out, or they have no network coverage. According to these researchers, about two-thirds of the British public are nomophobic. The "phobia" here is perhaps somewhat exaggerated, but we can still certainly recognize the symptoms.

Young adults between the ages of eighteen and twenty-four are the most likely to suffer from this affliction, with 77 percent admitting to being unable to part with their phones for even a few minutes. Another survey found that 22 percent of people would rather give up their toothbrush than their cell phone for an entire week, and a whopping 40 percent of iPhone users would rather have rotting teeth than give up their devices. Egads!

Obviously, this phobia is a direct result of our technologically saturated modern world. Not so long ago, there was no email, and all phones had to be plugged into the wall. If you weren't around to answer the phone, people left messages on home answering machines. You didn't expect to catch every call, and no one expected every call to be answered.

Today? We keep our phones in our pockets and use them constantly. It's the norm to be available 24/7. We expect messages and texts to be received and read immediately and for replies to come just as fast. The immediate gratification of all this connectivity is its own reward. We get used to constantly checking

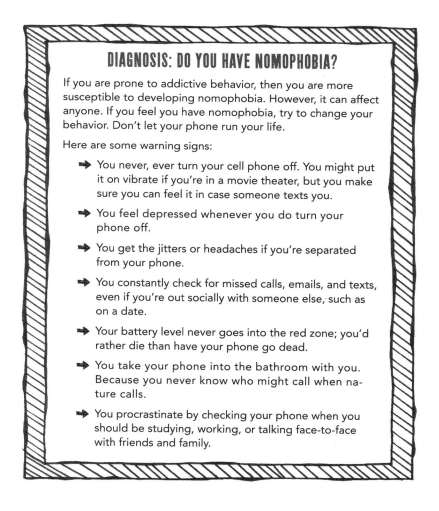

DIAGNOSIS: DO YOU HAVE NOMOPHOBIA?

If you are prone to addictive behavior, then you are more susceptible to developing nomophobia. However, it can affect anyone. If you feel you have nomophobia, try to change your behavior. Don't let your phone run your life.

Here are some warning signs:

➡ You never, ever turn your cell phone off. You might put it on vibrate if you're in a movie theater, but you make sure you can feel it in case someone texts you.

➡ You feel depressed whenever you do turn your phone off.

➡ You get the jitters or headaches if you're separated from your phone.

➡ You constantly check for missed calls, emails, and texts, even if you're out socially with someone else, such as on a date.

➡ Your battery level never goes into the red zone; you'd rather die than have your phone go dead.

➡ You take your phone into the bathroom with you. Because you never know who might call when nature calls.

➡ You procrastinate by checking your phone when you should be studying, working, or talking face-to-face with friends and family.

our cell phones to make sure we aren't missing anything, and we become anxious when we aren't constantly engaged in some back-and-forth.

While nomophobia results in anxious reactions common to all phobias, some psychologists believe that addiction is really at the heart of it. In any given day, we might receive hundreds of texts, calls, emails, and Twitter and Facebook alerts. Perhaps only a fraction of those messages is meaningful, but when one is, our brain releases a feel-good chemical called dopamine. Over time, we can become addicted to the rush we feel when we are constantly rewarded with texts and emails—then we become dependent on getting another fix, and our fear of not getting one is like a withdrawal symptom. There's a reason the Blackberry has been dubbed a Crackberry!

While the American Psychiatric Association doesn't formally recognize either nomophobia or cell-phone addiction, there is no question that this is a real and growing problem.

SCARE QUOTES

"I use my cell phone as much as I can—I talk to friends all the time. I'm like two thousand hours a month. It's crazy."
—Singer and actress Lisa Loeb

"Recently I was directing an episode of *Glee* and I lost my cell phone—and I didn't have time to buy a new one for three weeks. Well, the first few days I was anxious as hell, suffered the delirium tremens, didn't think I could make it through, etc. Then something kind of curious happened—I began to feel great."
—Actor and director Eric Stoltz

NOSOCOMEPHOBIA

FEAR OF HOSPITALS

The fear of hospitals is a fairly common medical phobia. Going to the E.R. is hardly anybody's idea of fun. Hospitals are expensive, and by definition, a visit means dealing with injury or illness, whether your own or someone else's. Most people find a way to get around or to overcome any hospital anxieties, since when it becomes medically necessary, there's no real choice except to go. What makes nosocomephobia particularly troubling and alarming, though, is that it can sometimes stop a person from getting the life-saving help they need. Someone with nosocomephobia may experience an extreme panic attack at the very idea of setting foot in a hospital—and so they refuse, no matter what.

Nosocomephobia is derived from the Greek word for "hospital," *nosokomeion*. While it is its own condition, it is also related to, or could be confused with, a number of other phobias, including fear of blood (hemophobia, page 85), fear of needles (trypanophobia, page 189), fear of illness (nosophobia), and fear of doctors (iatrophobia), among others. Indeed, fear of germs (mysophobia, page 104) and fear of death (thanatophobia, page 178) might feed a fear of hospitals. Being hospitalized, or even visiting someone in a hospital, is a vivid reminder that everyone dies, and that is scary and hard to deal with for anyone.

Many people develop a phobia about hospitals due to fears of medical mishaps. This is, unfortunately, not an unfounded concern. One recent study found that one-third of hospital patients are on the receiving end of mistakes or infections; after all, hospitals are filled with sick people, and despite a hospital's best efforts, those germs can spread. Still, most medical centers are excellent and quite safe, and if our wellness depends on their services, they are much better than the alternative of not going!

MÜNCHAUSEN SYNDROME

Curiously, there is a disorder that is the exact opposite of nosocomephobia: Münchausen syndrome. People with this disorder are addicted to hospitals—they can't get enough of them, and they will pretend to be sick just so that they can be admitted. It's thought that they have a deep-rooted craving for the attention and sympathy they get in the hospital. They'll happily undergo all sorts of treatments, including major surgery, to get the medical attention they crave. Their repeat trips to the hospital have earned them a special nickname among doctors and nurses: frequent flyers.

In addition to its associations with other phobias, nosocomephobia can be made worse by more prosaic issues. Some people don't like the smells and sounds of a hospital. And then there are the backless hospital gowns, the humiliation of bedpans, dealing with sick roommates, and their notoriously bad food. On top of that, patients are not in control of their environment—they are at the mercy of nurses, technicians, and aides who come and go unpredictably and at odd hours. While these are relatively minor inconveniences, and not usually the main concern of those with a phobia, they still strengthen the feeling that a hospital is not a place you want to be.

FAMOUS PHOBICS

A few months after Richard Nixon resigned the office of the presidency in disgrace, he developed a condition that caused serious swelling in his left leg. Doctors feared that he would develop a life-threatening blood clot, and they urged him to get treatment at a hospital. At first, he refused, fearing that he would not survive hospitalization. He finally gave in, though. He died—twenty years later.

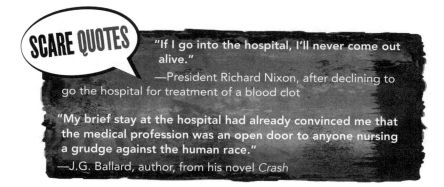

SCARE QUOTES

"If I go into the hospital, I'll never come out alive."

—President Richard Nixon, after declining to go the hospital for treatment of a blood clot

"My brief stay at the hospital had already convinced me that the medical profession was an open door to anyone nursing a grudge against the human race."

—J.G. Ballard, author, from his novel *Crash*

NYCTOPHOBIA

FEAR OF DARKNESS

F ear of the dark is quite common and probably natural. Children often develop a fear of the dark around the age of two. Most people outgrow their fear, but a surprising number of adults fess up to being afraid of the dark. Sleep researchers have found that people who are afraid of the dark are more likely to suffer from insomnia.

Little kids who develop nyctophobia (the term is from the Greek word *nyktos*, meaning "night") aren't usually afraid of monsters under the bed—not at first. Young children are most likely to associate darkness with separation from their parents. That's a scary thing. It's only as children grow older and their thinking becomes more sophisticated that they begin to imagine that they see or hear monsters, ghosts, or other bogeymen. The darkness provides a blank canvas onto which we can project our fears. And if we can't see it, who's to say it isn't there?

Night and darkness also loom large in symbolic and mythological ways, and these cultural understandings can help reinforce someone's belief that darkness is something to fear. Darkness is associated with evil and ignorance; the night, with the emergence of demons and spirits; and our personal "shadows" are the aspects of ourselves we regard negatively and try to hide.

Then, of course, on a practical level, nighttime can be more dangerous than the daytime. We are indeed more vulnerable to thieves and criminals if we're walking down poorly lit streets after dark. Fear and anxiety in this situation, however, is related to a credible threat; this is not nyctophobia. Indeed, what defines fear of the dark as a phobia is that it strikes us even when we know we are perfectly safe and there is no reason to be frightened.

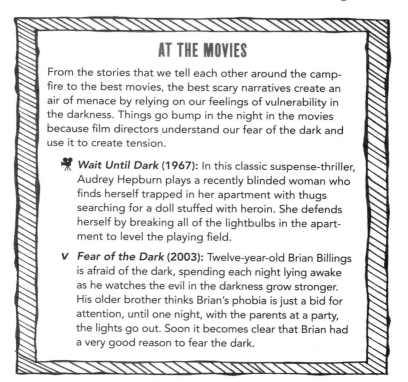

AT THE MOVIES

From the stories that we tell each other around the campfire to the best movies, the best scary narratives create an air of menace by relying on our feelings of vulnerability in the darkness. Things go bump in the night in the movies because film directors understand our fear of the dark and use it to create tension.

🎥 *Wait Until Dark* (1967): In this classic suspense-thriller, Audrey Hepburn plays a recently blinded woman who finds herself trapped in her apartment with thugs searching for a doll stuffed with heroin. She defends herself by breaking all of the lightbulbs in the apartment to level the playing field.

v *Fear of the Dark* (2003): Twelve-year-old Brian Billings is afraid of the dark, spending each night lying awake as he watches the evil in the darkness grow stronger. His older brother thinks Brian's phobia is just a bid for attention, until one night, with the parents at a party, the lights go out. Soon it becomes clear that Brian had a very good reason to fear the dark.

FAMOUS PHOBICS

Just because you fear the dark does not mean that you can't be incredibly brave. Burmese pro-democracy leader and Nobel Peace laureate Aung San Suu Kyi spent more than fifteen years in detention for speaking out against the military regime. And yet, she said, "I was a bit of a coward when I was small. I was terribly frightened of the dark."

British advice columnist Mariella Frostrup wrote about her fear of the dark for the newspaper the *Observer*, saying, "When I went public on my fear of the dark, writing 'me too' in what may have been one of my least helpful responses to a troubled reader, a deluge of sufferers wrote to admit they were similarly afflicted."

SCARE QUOTES

"Men fear death as children fear to go in the dark; and as that natural fear in children is increased by tales, so is the other."
—Francis Bacon, English philosopher

"Everyone is a moon, and has a dark side which he never shows to anybody."
—Mark Twain

"We can easily forgive a child who is afraid of the dark; the real tragedy of life is when men are afraid of the light."
—Plato

"Stars, hide your fires; Let not light see my black and deep desires."
—William Shakespeare, *Macbeth*

OBESOPHOBIA

FEAR OF BECOMING FAT

Many, if not most, people worry about their body image, and teenagers are especially susceptible to developing anxieties related to how they look. Obviously, teenagers are going through an accelerated period of great physical change, over which they have very little control. And the body-related anxiety that most often develops into a full-blown phobia, and that most often leads to a number of other serious problems, is the fear of becoming, or of being, fat. This affects both sexes, but it is particularly rampant among teenage girls.

Obesophobia (the term is from the Latin word *obesitas*, meaning "fatness") is sometimes referred to colloquially as weight phobia or fat phobia. People with this phobia often find that their desire to lose weight spirals out of control. They may exercise excessively and diet in unhealthy ways, sometimes avoiding any food that they think might cause them to gain weight. This can lead to life-threatening eating disorders such as anorexia and bulimia.

Sometimes this anxiety can develop because of an exaggerated response to genuine health concerns. In general, being overweight can cause health problems, and the more overweight a person is, the greater their risk for a host of ailments. In the United States, population-wide obesity rates are high; the Centers for Disease Control and Prevention estimates that more than one-third of US adults and about 17 percent of children and teens are obese. So there is an understandable concern that people overall should be taking better care of their health, in part by losing weight. Many times, a person may rationalize their phobia as simply being concerned with their health. However, this phobia, in the nature of all phobias, usually undermines effective habits and healthy attitudes, and sometimes it is entirely unrelated to a person's actual body weight or appearance. Someone with this phobia may or may not be genuinely overweight, and changes in their weight rarely calm the fear itself.

Instead, the phobia is more often instigated or made worse by a society-wide fat phobia. Cultural standards of beauty, especially for women, are epitomized by the American socialite Wallis Simpson, who once famously said, "A woman can't be too rich or too thin." In US society, fat shaming is rampant. There is a tremendous amount of pressure on women to be thin. We see it everywhere: Most models are rail-thin, and photos of movie stars are photoshopped to make them look even more svelte than they already are. Supermarket tabloids regularly feature lurid photos of celebrity cellulite.

There is a great deal of stigma associated with being fat in our society. Further, obese kids and teens are often the targets of bullying and cruelty.

Overcoming obesophobia often involves a series of steps. The first is to understand that obesity is itself a complex issue. Genetics can predispose someone to being heavier, and even one's income can be a factor; studies show that poorer families tend to be more overweight than more well-off families. A family's wealth or income can affect the type of food they eat, the amount of exercise they get, and so on. Thus, being overweight is not solely a matter of an individual's willpower, diet, or love of food.

The other step is practicing self-acceptance. In cases of a weight phobia, a person often needs the help of a counselor or therapist, since it can be hard to impossible to shift ingrained anxieties or beliefs on one's own. By practicing self-acceptance, you ideally reach a place where you love the body and person you are. If that means that your body doesn't fit the societal stereotype, so be it; if that means you'd prefer to weigh less than you currently do, that's fine, too.

SCARE QUOTES

"Even when someone gets to looking like she should be so proud of herself, she's like, 'I could be another three pounds less; I could be a little taller and have bigger lips.' Where does it end? . . . You just have to say, 'It's pretty damn good. I am right here at this moment and I'm OK with it. I've got other things to think about.'"

—Actress Melissa McCarthy

"I enjoy being me; I always have done. I've seen people where it rules their lives, you know, who want to be thinner or have bigger boobs, and how it wears them down. And I just don't want that in my life."

—Singer and songwriter Adele

"There would be all kinds of weird challenges to deal with that I don't have to deal with now. I don't want to go through life wondering if people are talking to me because I have a big rack. Not being the babest person in the world creates a nice barrier. The people who talk to you are the people who are interested in you. It must be a big burden in some ways to look that way and be in public!"

—Actress Lena Dunham, on being asked, "If you woke up tomorrow in the body of a Victoria's Secret model, what would you do for the rest of the day?"

"I don't want to be a supermodel; I want to be a role model."
—Queen Latifah, actress and singer

OPHIDIOPHOBIA

FEAR OF SNAKES

I f you're afraid of snakes, you have a lot of company: The fear of snakes is nearly universal, among humans and animals alike. Of course, most people have little or no contact with snakes, much less poisonous snakes. Nor do snakes pose much threat to humans, even when they are encountered. So what gives?

There is some pretty good scientific evidence that we are hardwired to fear snakes. Very large snakes—which tend to stun and immobilize their victims, then swallow them whole—and poisonous snakes are among the handful of ancient predators who likely posed a real threat to early humans. In evolutionary terms, avoiding snakes probably became a reflexive habit; seeing a snake, our ancestors probably didn't stop to consider whether it was poisonous or otherwise deadly. They just ran away.

Whether this wholly explains things or not, an ancient fear of (and respect for) snakes slithered its way into religion, myths, legends, and folktales—and into our subconscious. In Greek mythology, the monster Medusa sported snakes instead of hair. Gazing directly upon her would cause regular mortals to turn to stone. Throughout the world, in many different cultures, the

BAD SNAKE: SERPENTS IN POPULAR CULTURE

Snakes remain a potent symbol of malevolence and evil in popular culture today. Need a go-to scare, or want to signal the presence of a really bad guy? Enter the snake. Here is a list of some ways snakes appear:

🎥 ***The Jungle Book* (1967):** If movies with real snakes are too much, one could do worse than a little stroll down memory lane and watch *The Jungle Book*. Kaa, an Indian python, uses his hypnotic eyes to try to trap Mowgli in his coils and devour him. "Please, go to sleep, sleep tight little man-cub, rest in peace . . . sleep . . . sleep . . ."

🎥 ***Sssssss* (1973):** This mad-scientist/horror throwback features a herpetologist named Dr. Stoner (this movie was made in the early seventies, remember) who is intent on creating a human-snake hybrid that he is convinced will survive future environmental catastrophes. By most accounts, it's not a very good movie, but this opening credit is enough to give any ophidiophobe the shivers: "We wish to thank the cast and crew for their courageous efforts while being exposed to extremely hazardous conditions."

🎥 ***Raiders of the Lost Ark* (1981):** Known ophidiophobe Indiana Jones (played by Harrison Ford) descends into a pit of snakes and comes face-to-face with a cobra. In the director's cut, Steven Spielberg notes that they started with a few thousand harmless snakes, but then they had to add more. The only actual venomous snake on the set was the cobra. Great snake scene! Still a great movie!

🎥 ***Anaconda* (1997):** A deranged snake hunter (played by Jon Voight, who knows a thing or two about playing crazy guys) takes a documentary-film crew hostage on the Amazon River. He forces them to help him hunt down and capture the giant—and deadly—green anaconda he has been tracking. They find it, all right. Do they ever.

🎥 ***Snakes on a Plane* (2006):** If you happen to be on a plane where a bunch of poisonous snakes escape from the cargo hold and into the main cabin, your only hope is that a bad*ss like Samuel L. Jackson is on board to deal with the situation. Famous quote: "Enough is enough! I've had it with these motherf**king snakes on this motherf**king plane!" [Alternate quote for TV: "Enough is enough! I've had it with these monkey-fighting snakes on this Monday-through-Friday plane!"]

DEBUNKING THE HOOP SNAKE AND OTHER TALL SNAKE TALES

Not only do evil snakes crop up in myths and legends, but many legends have arisen to make snakes sound worse than they are. One of the more famous tall tales involves the "hoop snake," which is said to stick its tail in its mouth and roll like a wheel at high speeds after its prey, especially if it is going downhill. It has a venomous stinger on the end of its tail. When it reaches its victim, it whips its tail out and delivers a deadly sting. Needless to say, there is no such thing as a hoop snake.

The coachwhip snake, which looks like a long, braided rope, is a real snake, but it's acquired legendary abilities. Some claim this snake will chase its victims down, wrap them up in its coils, and whip them to death with its tail. Then, for good measure, it sticks its tail up the victim's nose to see if they are still breathing. Obviously, no animal does this.

Meanwhile, some propose that milk snakes got their name because they attack cows for their milk. Also not true. Milk snakes do hang around barns, but that's because barns are cool and dark and tend to harbor mice—which milk snakes are quite fond of.

snake represents evil, harm, and destruction, as well as creativity, healing, and protection. Then, of course, the Christian Bible starts human history with the tale of how Satan disguised himself as a serpent and tempted Eve to taste the forbidden fruit of the tree of knowledge. As a result, Adam and Eve got kicked out of the Garden of Eden, and everything went downhill, fast. That is one powerful symbol!

Either because of or in addition to this, some people fear snakes because of the "ick" factor: They think snakes are slimy (they're not) and therefore disgusting. Ultimately, what those with ophidiophobia (the term is from the Greek word *ophis*, meaning "snake") fear most is being bitten, even though the closest most of us ever come to snakes is viewing them through a Plexiglas window in a zoo.

As with many of the specific phobias in this book, ophidiophobia is effectively treated with the relaxation, desensitization, and cognitive behavioral therapies described in "Overcoming the Fear" (page 199).

FAMOUS PHOBICS

The things actors do to be in the movies. Apparently, Matt Damon cried "like a baby and rock[ed] back and forth when the snakes were spread all over the set of *We Bought a Zoo,*" costar Scarlett Johansson once told *People* magazine. Damon admitted to his fear of snakes, and he said that Johansson's teasing helped him deal with the slithery creatures.

And as mentioned before, one of the most famous ophidiophobics is Indiana Jones, who can face with aplomb just about any danger or threat—except, of course, for snakes.

SCARE QUOTES

"Yes, reason has been a part of organized religion, ever since two nudists took dietary advice from a talking snake."
—Jon Stewart

"Snakes. Why'd it have to be snakes?"
—Indiana Jones, *Raiders of the Lost Ark* (1981), upon peering into the snake-filled Well of Souls

"Don't touch me; I'm full of snakes."
—Jack Kerouac

"A tiger can smile / A snake will say it loves you/ Lies make us evil."
—Chuck Palahniuk (*Fight Club*)

ORNITHOPHOBIA

L ike several other animal phobias, fear of birds is often traced to a bad, traumatic experience someone had with a bird, especially in childhood. Perhaps a seagull swooped in and stole food from a child's hand, aggressive geese chased them (which has happened to me!), pigeons pooped on their head (which, for some reason, is supposed to be good luck), or a confused swallow got caught in the house and caused an uproar—all of these things have been known to trigger ornithophobia.

Further, while some anxiety about birds is common enough, people with true ornithophobia (the term is from the Greek word *ornitho*, meaning "bird") are distinguished by the severity of their reaction: They may find themselves unable to go on a picnic to the park, visit pet stores, or even in some cases leave their homes.

Cultural superstitions can play a role in feeding someone's ornithophobia. In ancient religions, birds were sometimes considered to have a special connection with the spirit world. They might be messengers for the gods, and they were used in divination or fortune telling. Though birds might not themselves be regarded as evil, they might represent negative omens.

Then again, certain birds have developed bad reputations, such as scavengers like vultures, and there are species-specific phobias, like alektorophobia, or fear of chickens. The raven, with its hunched black form and beady eyes, has long been associated with pain, misery, and death. It was no coincidence that it was a raven that came "rapping, rapping" on the chamber door in Edgar Allen Poe's famous poem "The Raven."

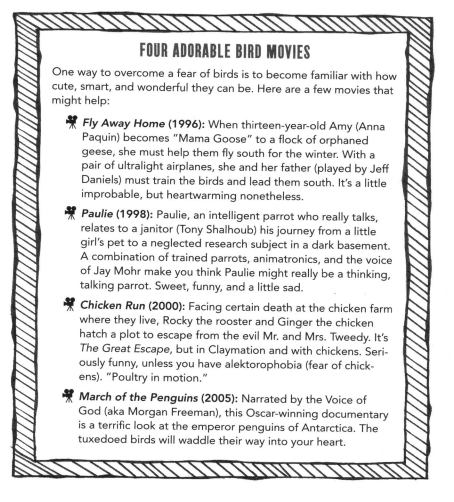

FOUR ADORABLE BIRD MOVIES

One way to overcome a fear of birds is to become familiar with how cute, smart, and wonderful they can be. Here are a few movies that might help:

- *Fly Away Home* (1996): When thirteen-year-old Amy (Anna Paquin) becomes "Mama Goose" to a flock of orphaned geese, she must help them fly south for the winter. With a pair of ultralight airplanes, she and her father (played by Jeff Daniels) must train the birds and lead them south. It's a little improbable, but heartwarming nonetheless.

- *Paulie* (1998): Paulie, an intelligent parrot who really talks, relates to a janitor (Tony Shalhoub) his journey from a little girl's pet to a neglected research subject in a dark basement. A combination of trained parrots, animatronics, and the voice of Jay Mohr make you think Paulie might really be a thinking, talking parrot. Sweet, funny, and a little sad.

- *Chicken Run* (2000): Facing certain death at the chicken farm where they live, Rocky the rooster and Ginger the chicken hatch a plot to escape from the evil Mr. and Mrs. Tweedy. It's *The Great Escape*, but in Claymation and with chickens. Seriously funny, unless you have alektorophobia (fear of chickens). "Poultry in motion."

- *March of the Penguins* (2005): Narrated by the Voice of God (aka Morgan Freeman), this Oscar-winning documentary is a terrific look at the emperor penguins of Antarctica. The tuxedoed birds will waddle their way into your heart.

FAMOUS PHOBICS

Lucille Ball, the great comedic actress, hated and feared birds. Her earliest memory registered when she was three years old, the day of her father's death. She remembered a bird that flew in the window, a picture that fell off the wall, the doctor's visit, and her mother's weeping. It left such an impression on her that she developed a lifelong phobia of birds. As an adult, she refused to stay in a hotel that displayed pictures of birds, and she would not allow any bird figures on the set of her television show. When she discovered that the very expensive wallpaper she had installed in her Beverly Hills home had shadowy images of birds, she had it ripped out and replaced with bird-free wallpaper.

Rapper Eminem supposedly suffers from a fear of owls, and the actress Scarlett Johansson told the *New York Post* that she is scared of birds. "Something about wings and beaks and flapping," she said. "I'm terrified of them. That still hasn't gone away. My uncle is terrified of birds, as well, so it runs in the family." And this is the actress who gave Matt Damon a hard time for his fear of snakes! (See "Ophidiophobia," page 124.)

However, it's only an urban legend that actress Tippi Hedren hates birds. She played the ingenue in the scariest film about birds ever made, *The Birds* (1963), by Alfred Hitchcock. During filming, bird trainers hurled ravens, gulls, and pigeons at Hedren, simulating the various bird attacks that appear in the film, and afterward she was said to be forever afraid of them. But she said recently, "I really like birds. Everyone always wants me to say that I can't stand to go near them. . . . Well, I'm sorry to disappoint you."

SCARE QUOTES

"He's up on the roof with his boids. He keeps boids. Dirty . . . disgusting . . . filthy . . . lice-ridden boids. You used to be able to sit out on the stoop like a person. Not anymore! No, sir! Boids! You get my drift?"

—Madelyn Cates, as the "concierge" in the 1968 film *The Producers*

"Birds . . . scream at the top of their lungs in horrified hellish rage every morning at daybreak to warn us all of the truth. They know the truth. Screaming bloody murder all over the world in our ears, but sadly we don't speak bird."

—Kurt Cobain

"We ate the birds. We ate them. We wanted their songs to flow up thorugh our throats and burst out of our mouths, and so we ate them. We wanted their feathers to bud from our flesh. We wanted their wings, we wanted to fly as they did, soar freely among the treetops and the clouds, and so we ate them."

—Margaret Atwood

PARASITOPHOBIA

Do you have a gnawing fear that something is sucking the life out of you? You may have parasitophobia—the fear of parasites. It's easy to understand this particular phobia. Parasites live in or on their unwilling hosts, taking nutrients and giving nothing in return. (It's no coincidence that we describe people who appear to be freeloading as leeches.) There's something that seems inherently unfair about the whole living arrangement. Plus, we know that some parasites can cause unpleasant and sometimes even life-threatening diseases, from malaria to severe diarrhea. Parasitic diseases are a huge problem in many developing nations.

There are plenty of reasons to fear parasites, but as usual, that fear becomes a phobia when it becomes blown all out of proportion and interferes with our everyday lives. Say you once heard that a friend of a friend got a leech while swimming in a lake, and now you refuse to even go near a lake. That's a fear turned phobia, because chances are slim that you, too, will find a leech clinging to your leg. Plus, leeches in general are pretty harmless. Sometimes, they're even beneficial; doctors have rediscovered the practice of using leeches to help heal skin grafts by removing excess blood and restoring circulation in blocked veins.

There is a specific phobia about becoming infected with parasitic worms, or helminths—helminthophobia. The eggs of these parasitic worms can contaminate water, food, and even our pets. They normally set up shop in our intestines. People with this phobia may worry about eating pork, because in the past it was known to carry a worm that caused a serious disease called trichinosis. (Trichinosis has been pretty much eliminated in pork in this country.)

BRAINWASHED BY A PARASITE

For obvious reasons, rats are not normally besties with cats. They normally become very timid if they smell cat urine. Unless, that is, they have become infected with a very sneaky parasite, a single-celled organism called *Toxoplasma gondii*. Infected rats become bold, even going to far as to approach cats, because the parasite activates a part of the rat's brain involved in sexual attraction. The rat is drawn to his main predator—call it Fatal Attraction—and soon becomes cat food. It is a wickedly clever way for the parasite to get inside of cats, which is the only place they can reproduce.

T. gondii can also infect humans—usually when people scoop out their cat's litter boxes. Experts estimate that between 30 and 50 percent of the world's population is infected with the parasite. Until fairly recently, the infection was thought to be fairly harmless, except for people with weak immune systems and pregnant women (it can be dangerous to newborn infants). But recent studies have found a link between *T. gondii* infection and schizophrenia, depression, and anxiety, as well as risk-taking behavior.

Should you get rid of your cat? Experts say no. Indoor cats don't pose a threat, and outdoor cats shed the parasite for only three weeks in their lives. Just make sure to keep surfaces like tables and counters where cats might walk clean—good basic hygiene.

Ticks are another story—in many parts of the country, they are a real problem. While the tick itself doesn't cause disease, it can transmit bacteria that cause Lyme disease, Rocky Mountain spotted fever, and other nasty ailments. It's just good sense to take measures to avoid tick bites—sticking to the trails rather than wading into high grassy areas while hiking, for example, or wearing long pants and long-sleeved shirts sprayed with a tick repellent. Someone with a tick phobia, on the other hand, might fear going camping or even going outdoors during the warm months of the year.

For some, parasitophobia is triggered by feelings of disgust, but it's far more common for people to develop the phobia after being bitten or infected with a parasite. They may become preoccupied with the notion that they may come down with some terrible disease, or suffer from the same experience all over again.

PARASITES IN POP CULTURE

Delusional parasitosis may be rare in real life, but you wouldn't know that from books and movies. The syndrome has made appearances in the TV series *The X-Files* and *House* (Dr. House himself is diagnosed as having delusional parasitosis). The motto of the Springfield Psychiatric Center in *The Simpsons* is "Because There May Not Be Bugs on You." Neil Gaiman's *The Sandman* and Philip K. Dick's *A Scanner Darkly* both have characters that suffer from delusional parasitosis. It's enough to make your skin crawl, really.

Parasites have been infecting our books and movies for some time now. Authors and filmmakers use our fears of being invaded, devoured from within, or perhaps forced to do the bidding of the alien. It's all about losing control of our destinies.

- 🎥 *The African Queen* (1951): This classic movie features an uneasy scene in which Charlie (played by Humphrey Bogart) emerges from the river, covered with leeches.

- 🎥 *Alien* (1979): Perhaps the classic science fiction-horror film featuring a nasty parasitic alien. All is fine—until the alien bursts out of its host's chest.

- 🎥 *Peeps* (2005): This novel by Scott Westerfield is about a parasite that causes people to become cannibalistic and repelled by those that they once loved.

Most people with parasitophobia can overcome their fears using the techniques described in "Overcoming the Fear" (page 199), along with the help of a professional therapist.

There is a related condition called delusional parasitosis, or Ekbom's syndrome. People with this syndrome believe that they are infested with parasites—most often, they report that they can feel parasites crawling on or under their skin. They are not infected with parasites, but they often scratch and pick at their skin in attempts to rid themselves of the imagined invaders. Although the syndrome can be treated with antipsychotic drugs, people who suffer from this disease often refuse treatment because of their core conviction that they are in fact infected with parasites.

FAMOUS PHOBICS

During the making of *The African Queen,* a queasy Humphrey Bogart insisted on using rubber leeches in a scene where leeches attach themselves to him. Director John Huston wanted Bogart nervous, however, and brought a tank full of the slimy creatures to the studio. Bogart still won out and got his rubber leeches in the end.

SCARE QUOTES

"One thing in the world I hate: leeches. Filthy little devils."
—Humphrey Bogart, in *The African Queen*

"We humans are the greatest of earth's parasites."
—Martin H. Fischer

"Every man has inside of himself a parasitic being who is acting not at all to his advantage."
—William S. Burroughs

PEDIOPHOBIA

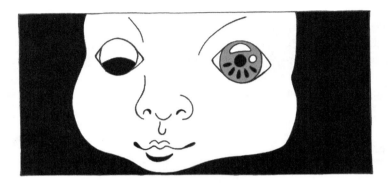

From the classic Raggedy Ann to the Katniss Everdeen Barbie, dolls are designed to serve as the beloved companions of childhood. They are intended as safe, heartwarming objects of affection. That benign purpose doesn't matter to someone with pediophobia, however. Nearly everyone has had the anxious experience of being creeped out by a particular doll, but someone with pediophobia tends to have that same uncanny experience with *all* dolls. The fear also often extends to other lifeless human figures, like ventriloquists' dummies, puppets, and mannequins.

As with many phobias, pediophobia—the term is from the Greek word *paidion,* meaning "little child," and not to be confused with "pedophobia," or the fear of children—often begins with a childhood experience: a big sister teasing a fearful younger sibling with a doll, perhaps. Or maybe just a certain doll that appeared particularly menacing. Whatever the cause, the reason for this fear in adulthood is probably related to the reason people usually love dolls as children: They mimic people, sometimes eerily so. One quintessential aspect of childhood play is to imagine dolls coming to life—and in this way, kids act out dreams and fantasies and re-create their everyday world, playing house and doctor. If a doll is something that is feared, however, this game can become terrifying. What would happen if a doll embodying what we feared most came to life? A whole genre of horror movies is based on this premise, in which this common childhood fantasy is turned inside out in the scariest possible ways.

In fact, there is probably something universal in this anxious response to inanimate figures that appear too humanlike. Robot designers and 3D computer animators talk about what they call the "uncanny valley." Up to a point, the more human-seeming a robot or a computer-animated character appears, the more appealing they will be. Until, that is, the likeness is *too* strong. When the resemblance to a real human face is so close as to be almost identical, people find it upsetting, strange, and possibly threatening. In a way, someone with pediophobia simply has a broader sense of that uncanny valley.

MEXICO CITY'S ISLAND OF THE DOLLS

Deep in a labyrinth of ancient Aztec canals in the southern part of Mexico City lies the Isla de las Muencas, or Island of the Dolls. Visitors can hire a boatman to pole a colorful gondola on a four-hour round trip to visit one of the world's creepiest tourist destinations. The island is home to hundreds of terrifyingly battered, decaying, and dirty dolls. The dolls—or sometimes just their heads or parts of their bodies—hang from trees and wires strung between trees. Their flesh has blistered in the sun, mold discolors the skin, and spiders and insects have taken up residence inside their bodies and what remains of their hair.

There is a story, of course: in the 1950s, the island's only inhabitant, Julián Santana Barrera, found the body of a drowned girl in the canal. He was haunted by her death, and so when he found a doll floating by in the canal, he hung it from a tree on the island, hoping to appease her soul and protect the island from evil spirits. Over the years, he accumulated more and more dolls. After about fifty years of collecting dolls and hanging them from the trees on his island, Julian was found dead—drowned, in the same spot where he'd found the girl. Or so the story goes. Today, the locals keep the island open to visitors—if they dare.

FAMOUS PHOBICS

Libba Bray, author of many young-adult novels, including *Beauty Queens* and *The Diviners*, is seriously afraid of dolls. When fellow author and friend Maureen Johnson took her to an American Girl doll store to help her get over her fear, Bray said, "You can't look it in the eyes. That's how it gets to you. You can't look it in the eyes."

Plenty of visitors to the Fort East Martello Museum, in Key West, Florida, can be creeped out by Robert the Haunted Doll, which was once owned by the painter and author Robert Eugene Otto. Legend has it that Eugene's parents mistreated a family maid who was skilled in black magic, who then put a curse on a doll that she gave to Eugene for his sixth birthday. Eugene loved the doll, and spent hours talking to it. The parents were convinced that the doll talked back. When Eugene went to sleep in his room at night, he would often awaken his family with screams of fright. His parents would find his furniture knocked over, and Eugene in bed, yelling, "Robert did it!"

SCARE QUOTES

"You know you've made it when you've been molded in miniature plastic. But you know what children do with Barbie dolls—it's a bit scary, actually."
—Cate Blanchett

"Dolls with no little girls around to mind them were sort of creepy under any conditions."
—Stephen King

PHOBOPHOBIA

FEAR OF PHOBIAS

It might be more accurate to say that phobophobia—the term is from the Greek word *phobos*, for "fear"—is the most generalized type of panic disorder. People with phobophobia believe that something terrible will happen if they allow themselves to feel afraid or anxious. It's thought that phobophobia is actually the underlying culprit behind both agoraphobia (page 26) and claustrophobia (page 57), in which the fear of having a panic attack becomes specific to a particular situation or circumstance.

Panic attacks are not unusual; experts say that millions of people experience them each

PAN CREATED THE FIRST PANIC

The word *panic* comes from the name of the Greek god Pan, which also means "all" in Greek. Pan was the half-goat, half-man deity who was in charge of the wild, shepherds, and their flocks. He was supposed to make sure that everything was fertile, and so it was only appropriate that he himself was a lusty fellow. He was also quite the party animal, and he was notorious for darting out of the woods and frightening mere mortals. He sent them into a panic, you might say, which is why the experience of sudden, unexpected fear goes by that name.

CULTURAL ANXIETY

In 1890, psychologist William James noted that we lead a cushy life compared with our ancestors, who were at the mercy of nature. "In civilized life, in particular," he wrote, "it has at last become possible for large numbers of people to pass from the cradle to the grave without ever having had a pang of genuine fear." And yet, surveys consistently show that we are more anxious than ever before—perhaps because we have more time to worry.

Perhaps no one has done more to capture our cultural anxieties than Woody Allen, who has become legendary for his own fears. He's not afraid to use his anxieties to tell stories that resonate. His best, even after all these years, would still have to be *Annie Hall* (1977), in which he plays a neurotic New York comedian who falls in love with an equally neurotic woman from the Midwest.

The Sopranos, a TV series that ran from 1999 to 2007, tapped into the cultural anxieties of our time with the realistic portrayal of a mobster, Tony Soprano, who suffers from an anxiety disorder. The series opens with a scene in which Tony, played by the late James Gandalfini, suffers a panic attack while watching some ducks in his backyard pool.

Analyze This (1999) is a more light-hearted look at an anxiety-ridden mob boss. When an insecure gangster (played by Robert De Niro) begins to have panic attacks, he seeks the help of a psychiatrist (Billy Crystal).

year. About a third of people who have a panic attack go on to have another. It's the fear of having another panic attack that leads to developing a phobia.

Typically, what happens is that someone is out minding his or her own business when—POW!—out of the blue, the heart begins to pound and there's a shortness of breath and uncontrollable trembling. These are the hallmarks of the fight-or-flight response that overcome us when anxiety hits. But the thing about a panic attack is that it occurs suddenly, without any warning or seemingly any reason. Panic attacks are not dangerous, although people suffering panic attacks often feel as though they are having a heart attack, not to mention going crazy. The attacks don't usually last longer than twenty minutes—our bodies just can't keep up those symptoms for much longer.

There's no single trigger for panic attacks, though they usually appear during the teen or early-adult years, and women are more likely to have them. They are often connected with a stressful event, like moving, going to college, or starting a new job, or as a reaction to some kind of trauma. Experts believe that stressful events lower the trigger point at which anxiety—and its miserable physical symptoms—kick in.

OVERCOMING THE FEAR

If left untreated, phobophobia and panic disorder can lead to depression, substance abuse, and even attempted suicide. Fortunately, most people with phobophobia and panic disorders can be helped with professional therapy. See "Overcoming the Fear" (page 199), for some of the techniques that are often used, but for phobophobia, it's important to practice these with the help of a qualified professional. Learning how to relax through panic attacks is key, and therapists will sometimes prescribe antianxiety medications to help control the fear. Some people also find support groups to be helpful, whether groups meet face-to-face or online. Support groups can't take the place of therapy, but it's always good to know firsthand that you're not alone.

SCARE QUOTES

"So, first of all, let me assert my firm belief that the only thing we have to fear is fear itself—nameless, unreasoning, unjustified terror, which paralyzes needed efforts to convert retreat into advance."
—President Franklin D. Roosevelt, in his first inaugural address

"Anxiety is love's greatest killer. It makes others feel as you might when a drowning man holds on to you. You want to save him, but you know he will strangle you with his panic."
—Writer Anaïs Nin

POGONOPHOBIA

T hose screaming little kids who refuse to sit on Santa's lap? Don't be too hard on them. They might be suffering from pogonophobia—fear of beards (the term comes from the Greek word *pogon,* meaning "beard"). Pogonophobia is fairly common for children, and in fact, the phobia is usually confined to children (they tend to outgrow it as they get older).

For those who have it, it's all about fearing the strange or unfamiliar. The phobia tends to arise in young kids who have not been exposed to bearded men. If you're used to a clean-shaven Daddy, and all of a sudden somebody with a furry face confronts you—or worse, pulls you onto his lap for a little

THE PLAYOFF BEARD

If you're a hockey fan, you know April is a scraggly time. Since the 1980s, it is common practice for hockey players to not shave until their team either wins the Stanley Cup or is eliminated from post-season play. Many male fans join in, which no doubt leads many spouses and significant others—not to mention any pogonophobic children—to breathe a sigh of relief when hockey season is over.

Christmas chat—it can be intimidating and frightening. If your father has a beard, however, it's unlikely that beards will inspire any negative associations.

What's more, in movies, television, and books, the bad guys are often (but not always) portrayed as bearded. There's something about a beard that says, "Don't mess with me."

A BEARDED HALL OF FAME

Abraham Lincoln: His is one of the most famous beards of all time, but he wasn't always bewhiskered. Lincoln was running for president in the fall of 1860 when eleven-year-old Grace Bedell wrote the candidate a letter, saying, "I have got 4 brothers, and part of them will vote for you any way and if you let your whiskers grow I will try and get the rest of them to vote for you. You would look a great deal better for your face is so thin. All the ladies like whiskers and they would tease their husbands to vote for you and then you would be President." At first, Lincoln demurred, but he eventually decided to grow a beard, perhaps to cover up his famously scrawny neck and sunken cheeks.

➡ **Guitarist Billy F. Gibbons and bassist Dusty Hill from the band ZZ Top:** These rockers have been wearing their signature chest-length beards since the 1970s. Ironically, the band's drummer, Frank Beard, is clean-shaven.

➡ **Yosemite Sam:** This Looney Tunes character's beard and moustache cover every bit of his face, except for his eyes, ears, and nose.

➡ **Bluebeard:** Charles Perrault published this famous French folktale in 1697. It's about a rich nobleman who had a blue beard, which made him so ugly that all the women and girls ran away from him.

➡ **Wes Bentley as Seneca Crane in *The Hunger Games* (2012):** The head Gamemaker's elaborately sculpted beard even has its own Facebook fan page!

➡ **Johnny Depp as Captain Jack Sparrow in *Pirates of the Caribbean* (2003):** Sparrow's braided, beaded twin-goatee beard also has its own Facebook fan page!

LITTLE ALBERT

In 1920, in a study that would be considered unethical to-day, psychologist John B. Watson created a beard phobia in a nine-month-old boy named Little Albert. He exposed Little Albert to a number of furry things, including a white rat. Little Albert was fine with the white rat, until—bang!—Watson frightened the child with a loud noise. After doing this a few times, Watson found that he could make the tyke cry just by showing him the rat. After that, Little Albert was afraid of many furry things—including Watson himself wearing a Santa Claus mask.

It's not clear what happened to poor Little Albert after that, but it's a good bet that he suffered from a fear of psychologists for a long time.

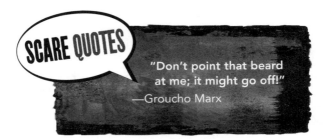

SCARE QUOTES

"Don't point that beard at me; it might go off!"
—Groucho Marx

PYROPHOBIA

FEAR OF FIRE

I t is perfectly normal and healthy to be cautious around fire and to regard uncontrolled fires as something to fear and guard against. Our distant ancestors understood that fire could be both useful and dangerous, and a healthy respect for its power seems hardwired into us. However, people with pyrophobia (the term comes from the Greek word *pyro,* meaning "fire") fear even well-controlled, small fires. They become overly anxious about even the possibility that a fire might break out. There's no roasting marshmallows over the campfire or cuddling in front of a blazing fireplace. Even birthday candles can be terrifying. Those with pyrophobia may become afraid to leave home because they fear that only a pile of smoldering ashes will be waiting when they return. They constantly worry that their smoke detectors will not work correctly if a fire happens at night when they are asleep, so they may be troubled by insomnia.

Typically, pyrophobia develops in response to a frightening experience with fire. Obviously, watching a house or any other structure go up in flames can be very traumatic, particularly if someone dies. Not only is it a very dangerous situation to witness, but it also makes us aware of how little power we have against an out-of-control fire.

145

Throughout history, fire has burned itself into our brains, so to speak, as something both sacred and evil. In many traditions, fire was a test of power or purity. In the Bible, God manifested himself to Moses in the form of a burning bush, and hell is famously a place of fire and brimstone. In medieval times, fire was also a common method of executing people convicted of witchcraft. It is perhaps no surprise that some of the most fearsome mythical creatures are fire-breathing dragons!

Pyrophobia is effectively treated using the techniques described in "Overcoming the Fear" (page 199), along with the help of a therapist. Since fire really is a potential threat in our everyday lives, it may help to go to a fire safety seminar or tour a fire department. You'll feel better equipped to anticipate and deal with any fire hazards that surround you.

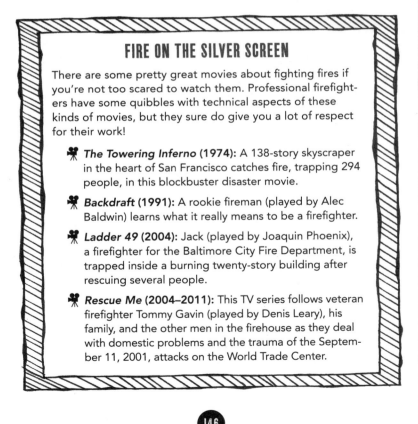

FIRE ON THE SILVER SCREEN

There are some pretty great movies about fighting fires if you're not too scared to watch them. Professional firefighters have some quibbles with technical aspects of these kinds of movies, but they sure do give you a lot of respect for their work!

- *The Towering Inferno* (1974): A 138-story skyscraper in the heart of San Francisco catches fire, trapping 294 people, in this blockbuster disaster movie.

- *Backdraft* (1991): A rookie fireman (played by Alec Baldwin) learns what it really means to be a firefighter.

- *Ladder 49* (2004): Jack (played by Joaquin Phoenix), a firefighter for the Baltimore City Fire Department, is trapped inside a burning twenty-story building after rescuing several people.

- *Rescue Me* (2004–2011): This TV series follows veteran firefighter Tommy Gavin (played by Denis Leary), his family, and the other men in the firehouse as they deal with domestic problems and the trauma of the September 11, 2001, attacks on the World Trade Center.

FAMOUS PHOBICS

Hans Christian Andersen became pyrophobic after a good friend died in a fire aboard a steamship as it was crossing the Atlantic Ocean. After that, he always carried a rope with him in case a fire forced him to escape through a window. Ironically, one of his most famous stories is "The Little Match Girl," in which a poor, freezing girl tries to sell matches on the street. She keeps herself warm by lighting matches, and sees in their flames lovely visions of a happier life. She freezes to death after she runs out of matches.

SCARE QUOTES

"A spark neglected makes a mighty fire."
—English poet Robert Herrick

"Remember in elementary school you were told that in case of fire you have to line up quietly in a single file from smallest to tallest? What is the logic in that? What, do tall people burn slower?"
—Warren Hutcherson, comedian

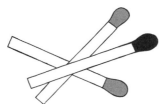

RADIOPHOBIA

FEAR OF RADIATION

L ike fear of fire, fear of radiation is a phobia that takes a genuine fear and concern—that radiation in large doses can be dangerous and deadly—and extends it to all situations, even those in which small, harmless doses of radiation are used in beneficial ways, like getting X-rays and other medical treatments involving radiation. In this way, like many phobias, radiophobia—the Latin word *radiatio* means "shining" or "radiation"—causes all sorts of problems because a person can't distinguish true risk from imagined risk.

We tend to fear things we don't understand, and radiation certainly plays into that anxiety over the unknown. You can't see it, smell it, or taste it (although you sometimes feel it—the sun's warm rays are a form of radiation). Many people associate radiation with horrific events, like the dropping of atomic bombs in World War II, the meltdown of the Chernobyl nuclear power plant in Russia in 1986, and the nuclear power plant disasters in Japan following the earthquake and tsunami of 2011. Indeed, these are just the sorts of traumatic events that spark phobias. Ever since World War II, the idea that radiation creates monstrous mutations has made its way into countless comic books, TV shows, and movies—from *Godzilla* to the *Teenage Mutant*

Ninja Turtles to *Spider-Man* and *The Hulk*. Further, almost daily, we hear news reports questioning the safety of much lower-level radiation exposure: in cell phones, airport security scanners, power lines, dental X-rays, and more. But what's really dangerous, and what's not?

BEFORE WE KNEW BETTER

In the early days, people were fascinated with radioactivity—but they didn't necessarily understand what it could do. Manufacturers put radioactive materials in face cream, toothpaste, and water and promised that it would beautify, rejuvenate, and purify. Of course, we understand the dangers of radiation today and use it with appropriate caution and respect.

Marie Curie (1867–1934) discovered not one but two radioactive elements—and actually coined the word *radioactive*—and she earned the first Nobel Prize ever awarded to a woman. She was such a scientific rock star that she then earned another Nobel in a different field. Unfortunately, nobody at the time was very aware of the health risks of radiation, and Madame Curie was no different. She didn't take any protective measures. In fact, she used to carry test tubes filled with radioactive material in the pockets of her lab coat. She died of a blood disease, which was almost certainly caused by her long-term exposure to radiation.

Marie Curie and her husband, Pierre, discovered that radium has several notable qualities, one of which is that it destroys cancer cells (which is one beneficial use today). Another is that it glows in the dark. This gave watchmakers a brilliant idea: they could use radium-laced paint to create watches that glow in the dark. This would be just the thing for US soldiers fighting in World War I. The glowing paint was considered harmless by the company and by the hundreds of women who painted the watch faces, and it was fun to play with. The women also painted their fingernails and teeth with the stuff. Years later, all the company's "radium girls" began developing serious health problems and diseases, of which they eventually died, caused by their exposure to radium. Sadly, their experience is one reason why radioactive materials are handled with such caution today.

The truth is, there are many different kinds of radiation, both natural and artificial. Put simply, radiation is energy. Lower-energy radiation is mostly emitted in the form of waves, like radio waves, microwaves, and ultraviolet waves. These forms of radiation can be harmful (that is, causing cancer and other diseases) in very heavy or long-term doses. We are still learning what amounts and levels are safe, but, for instance, this is now why you should wear sunblock and avoid excessive or regular tanning.

Other forms of radiation can have so much energy that they can do serious damage to cells and their DNA. They're everywhere, from cosmic rays from the sun and stars to bananas. That's right. Bananas (and other potassium-rich foods) give off small amounts of radiation in the form of high-energy gamma rays.

Which leads to the final point: Radiation is everywhere. Though it may be hard for someone with radiophobia to contemplate, radiation is in the air, the ground, the water, our food, and even our bodies. It's called natural-background radiation, and it's perfectly safe. Small amounts of radiation are usually not even noticeable. Our bodies repair any cellular damage quickly, and we go on with life as usual.

OVERCOMING THE FEAR

Educate yourself about the relative risks of radiation sources. This is one of those cases in which knowledge can really help. Sensible caution is wise, and there are easy ways to limit your exposure to everyday sources of radiation. Avoiding medically necessary X-rays, however, is *not* one of them. As with all phobias, if anxiety and panic can't be managed on your own, work with a therapist.

Here are some brief tips for dealing with three everyday sources of radiation: cell phones, cigarettes, and microwave ovens.

Cell Phones

Cell phones emit radio-frequency radiation, and people who spend a lot of time on their cell phone have begun to worry about the long-term effects of holding a phone on your ear. Simply put, to be safe, create more distance.

Hold your phone about a pencil's width away from your ear when you are using it. Better yet, use a hands-free device or put it in speaker mode. You can also text more and call less.

Also, dial with your phone on speaker. The radio-frequency radiation is strongest when your phone is attempting to make a call, so hold it away from your head until someone picks up. Then, switch the phone from one ear to another as you talk.

Smoking

Did you know that tobacco smoke contains the radiation that is naturally absorbed by tobacco plants? You already know that tobacco smoke contains a boatload of cancer-causing chemicals, so do yourself a favor: Don't smoke.

Microwave Ovens

Microwave ovens use electromagnetic radiation. Microwaves are not radioactive, and they don't change food; they only make it hot! The only real concern with microwaves, beyond being cautious when handling hot food, is to make sure that the door to your microwave oven seals properly. Otherwise, some microwaves might leak out, and if you were standing right next to the appliance, these could heat the cells in your body. To avoid even this small amount of microwave exposure, simply don't stand directly in front of an operating microwave.

SCARE QUOTES

"We must not forget that when radium was discovered no one knew that it would prove useful in hospitals."

—Marie Curie

SELACHOPHOBIA

FEAR OF SHARKS

When it comes to selachophobia, it's fair to ask, Who *isn't* afraid of sharks? Humans have developed a number of well-earned fears regarding other predators (like snakes, see "Ophidiophobia," page 124), and sharks are often regarded as the ultimate predator. They are often portrayed as nothing but a mouth full of very sharp teeth and a bottomless appetite.

What distinguishes those with selachophobia is that their fear of sharks extends to any body of water anywhere. They don't just avoid the ocean, but they'll refuse to swim in freshwater lakes, rivers, and sometimes even swimming pools. Their phobia imagines sharks where they can't possibly exist.

You might be surprised to learn that selachophobia is relatively new. The term comes from the Greek word *selachos*, meaning "shark," and the phobia is related to ichthyophobia (the term is from the Greek word *ichthus*), or fear of fish. Our ancestors weren't much in the habit of frolicking in the ocean, and so they didn't have the opportunity to hone their fear of sharks. They knew of them, and there were scattered tales of whalers and fishermen who witnessed fearsome shark attacks, but for the most part sharks didn't impact human life very much.

SWIMMING SMART

Overcoming selachophobia—and enjoying a summer day at the beach—is a matter of easing one's fear using the techniques in "Overcoming the Fear" (page 199) and following a few precautionary ocean-swimming guidelines. Contrary to popular myth, sharks almost never target humans; in most shark attacks, they mistake a human for their preferred food (fish and seals). However, by swimming smart, you minimize to almost nothing the already infinitesimal chance of encountering a shark.

Here is what you can do:

1. Stay in a group; sharks avoid groups and focus on individuals.

2. Stay close to shore.

3. Stay out of the water during the twilight hours and at night, when sharks are most active.

4. Don't wear shiny jewelry—a shark might mistake it for fish scales.

5. Don't enter the water if you are bleeding—sharks have a great sense of smell.

That all changed in 1916. Bathing in the ocean had only recently become a popular pastime. People flocked to the New Jersey shore in droves that summer, hoping to escape a deadly heat wave and polio epidemic. But then a rogue shark or sharks (it's still not clear how many were involved) began attacking people. One attack even took place in a creek that flowed into the sea. In a twelve-day period, five people were attacked; only one survived. A media frenzy erupted, and sharks ever after became known as vicious, bloodthirsty man-eating machines.

In 1974, inspired by the 1916 shark attacks, author Peter Benchley published *Jaws,* a novel about a great white shark that terrorizes a fictional coastal community. Director Steven Spielberg adapted it as a terrifying movie the following year. Together, these two artists almost single-handedly established selachophobia as an enduring modern phenomenon.

SHARK BAIT

Sharks: they're big, they have sharp teeth, and they are not our friends. While none of these movies can live up to *Jaws* for sheer cultural impact, these are memorable.

🎥 ***Blue Water, White Death* (1971):** In this documentary, a film crew and team of divers travels the world in search of the great white shark. At first, they are content to film the sharks from inside protective cages, but when they enter the open water, things get really scary!

🎥 ***Deep Blue Sea* (1999):** Scientists in search of a cure for Alzheimer's disease accidentally create sharks that are bigger, stronger, smarter, and fiercer than ever before. Oh, scientists, when will you ever learn?

🎥 ***Open Water* (2003):** A couple on a Caribbean holiday go scuba diving, thinking they'll come back with some interesting stories to tell their friends. Do they ever. When their tour boat accidentally leaves them behind in the middle of the ocean, they must keep themselves safe in the midst of shark-infested waters. Based on a true story!

🎥 ***The Reef* (2010):** A group of friends capsize while sailing to a coral reef, only to find themselves stalked by a great white shark.

🎥 ***Sharknado* (2013):** You can imagine what went through the heads of the makers of this cheesy made-for-TV movie. "Sharks? Old news. Tornadoes? Been there, done that. Tornadoes made out of sharks? Awesome! Let's do it."

Since then, the news media has made a point of dramatically increasing the reporting of shark attacks, thus further feeding the fear of sharks. However, the attention given to shark attacks far outweighs the actual danger. Sharks attacks are very, very rare. You are more likely to be struck by lightning or crushed by a vending machine than to be bitten by a shark.

Will this statistic reassure those with selachophobia? Probably not. It's in the nature of phobias to ignore the probabilities and to focus solely on the possibility, however remote, that such a thing might happen at all.

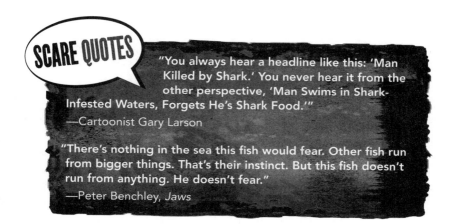

SCARE QUOTES

"You always hear a headline like this: 'Man Killed by Shark.' You never hear it from the other perspective, 'Man Swims in Shark-Infested Waters, Forgets He's Shark Food.'"
—Cartoonist Gary Larson

"There's nothing in the sea this fish would fear. Other fish run from bigger things. That's their instinct. But this fish doesn't run from anything. He doesn't fear."
—Peter Benchley, *Jaws*

SINISTROPHOBIA

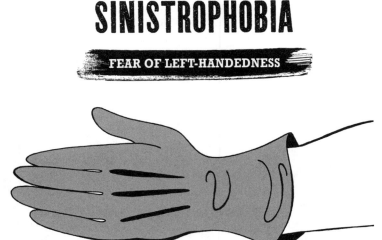

In a world dominated by right-handed people, lefties can feel
... well, a little left out. Most everyday objects, from scissors
to spiral-bound notebooks, are designed with right-handed
people in mind. But left-handed people today—roughly 10 percent
of the population—should still thank their lucky stars. After all,
things could be much worse—and they have been! Western culture
has long distrusted the left. An ancient Greek philosopher once
wrote, "The starting point is honorable, and above is more honorable than below, and front than back, and right than left." Several
centuries ago, being left-handed could get you accused of witchcraft and burned at the stake. A couple of generations ago, many
left-handed kids were punished for writing with their left hands.

While most people are no longer afraid of lefties, and this phobia
rarely arises as a problem anymore, there remains a deeply rooted
cultural bias against the left hand. This bias is the remnant of
folklore and old superstitions that once associated the left side
with evil and gave rise to the phobia to begin with.

Let's take language. The Latin word *sinister* originally just
meant "left," but it came to signify something evil or unlucky.
The word *left* itself comes from an Anglo-Saxon word meaning

"weak." In many modern languages, the word for "right" also means "correct" and is associated with justice and authority. If you've got two left feet, you're a clumsy dancer, and a left-handed compliment is more of an insult. Even the Greek and Roman alphabets favored righties over lefties: Because we write from left to right, right-handed people can more easily see what they are writing and avoid smudging their work.

Then there are the superstitions. In ancient times, spilling salt was considered very bad luck (it was expensive!). But the evil spirits that liked to hang around your left shoulder were apparently greedy little devils, so you could buy them off by throwing a little salt over your left shoulder. An itchy right palm meant that you would receive money, while an itchy left palm meant—you guessed it—that you could kiss your money good-bye. The practice of wearing wedding rings on the third finger of the left hand began with the Greeks and Romans, who wore them to counteract the evil associated with the left hand.

Religion has hardly treated lefties any better. In both Judaism and Christianity, the right hand of God is the place to be. The Christian New Testament tells a parable in which a shepherd places his sheep (representing the righteous) on the right and the goats (the fallen) on the left. The sheep gambol about in heaven, while the goats go straight to hell. In Islam, the left hand is considered unclean. Etiquette in the Middle East and other nations is that you use the left hand for personal hygiene and the right for eating—no exceptions for lefties. Black magic and Satanism is sometimes referred to as the left-hand path.

Clearly, history has not been kind to left-handed people!

FAMOUS PHOBICS

Being left-handed actually may have some advantages. In our brains, the left hemisphere almost always handles language, logic, and speech, while the right hemisphere takes care of emotion and image processing. We know that the left hemisphere of the brain is dominant in right-handed people, but left-handed people don't show quite the same one-sided dominance. The brain hemispheres of most lefties aren't as specialized—and there is more "cross-talk" between the two sides of the brain. Scientists think that these differences may account for the fact that left-handed people tend to be more creative and have better hand-eye coordination and quicker reflexes.

Athletes

Left-handers are used to dealing with righties, but not the other way around, so facing left-handed opponents can throw off a righty's game. In Major League Baseball, 25 percent of players are southpaws. Left-handed batters can get a better angle on a ball thrown by a right-handed pitcher, and they're a couple of steps closer to first base. Most ballplayers find it harder to hit off of a left-handed pitcher. Lefties also have an advantage in tennis and boxing. Notable left-handed athletes: Babe Ruth, Sandy Koufax, Stan Musial, Andy Pettitte, David Wells, Randy Johnson, and Ted Williams (baseball); Martina Navratilova, John McEnroe, and Monica Seles (tennis); Oscar de la Hoya (boxing); Gayle Sayers, Steve Young, and Tim Tebow (football); and Pelé (soccer).

Presidents and Other Leaders

Some scientists think that left-handed people have an edge over righties in speaking skills. They're good at getting people to listen to them! Six of the last twelve US presidents have been left-handed: Harry S. Truman, Gerald Ford, Ronald Reagan (who was supposedly left-handed but forced by his teachers and parents to write with his right hand), George H. W. Bush, Bill Clinton, and Barack Obama. We haven't seen that many left-handed presidents before, but that may be because, in past generations, lefties were forced to use their right hands at an early age.

Other famous left-handed leaders: Winston Churchill, Napoleon Bonaparte, Charlemagne, Alexander the Great, and Mahatma Gandhi.

Scientists

Those lefty creative thinking skills come in handy for scientists. Marie Curie and her husband, Pierre, were both left-handed, and historians believe their daughter and her husband (also Nobel Prize winners) were left-handed as well. Alan Turing, the father of computer science, was left-handed.

Artists

One of the most creative thinkers of all time, Leonardo da Vinci, was a southpaw. He was a prolific inventor and scientist, but he may be best known for his painting known as the *Mona Lisa*. Some experts suggest that his lefty brain helped him read and capture her mysterious smile. Other famous left-handed painters include Michelangelo, Raphael, and M. C. Escher. Mozart, Jimi Hendrix, Bob Dylan, Sting, and Lauryn Hill are among the many famous left-handed musicians.

Criminals

Of course, not all lefties are awesome and wonderful people. Many famous criminals were left-handed, including Jack the Ripper, Billy the Kid, John Dillinger, Albert Henry DeSalvo (the Boston Strangler), and Osama bin Laden. A sign, perhaps, that you do not want to mess with left-handers.

SCARE QUOTES

"The left half of the brain is dominant in right-handed people, and the right half is dominant in left-handed people. And that's why left-handed people are the only ones in their right minds."
—Bob Thaves, from the comic strip *Frank and Ernest*

"When I was a kid I seemed to do everything from back to front. I used to write backward, and every time the masters at my school looked at my book, they used to throw little fits. . . . I do everything with my left hand, and no matter how hard I try, I can't alter the habit."
—Sir Paul McCartney

"I think left-handed people tend to have a chip on their shoulder, and they've got something to prove."
—Broadcast journalist and lefty Ted Koppel

SOCIAL PHOBIA

SOCIAL ANXIETY DISORDER

W hat used to be known as social phobia is now most often called social anxiety disorder. Unlike the rest of the phobias in this book, this fear has no mystifying Greek or Latin name. It's just its own bad self, and it refers to the strong fear of being judged by others and being embarrassed in everyday social or performance situations.

Some people with social anxiety disorder feel anxious in nearly all social situations. Others struggle with specific situations, like eating in public places, speaking to strangers on the phone, or going on a date. This variety is one reason why many no longer consider it a phobia, since that implies avoidance of a particular object or situation, and this anxiety can crop up in almost any circumstance. In an uncomfortable social situation, a person is likely to blush, sweat, and shake. Worrying that people will notice their physical symptoms makes the person even more anxious. As a result, they may come to avoid any and all social situations as much as possible.

Social anxiety disorder is the most common of all anxiety disorders. Studies show that between 7 and 13 percent of people in the United States will have a problem with social anxiety at some point in their life. Social phobias usually begin in the teenage years; thirteen is the average age of onset. No mystery there: Adolescence, the transition to adulthood, is a time of great physical, social, and personal change. This makes us self-conscious and hyper-aware of what others think of us.

A social phobia is *not* just an extreme form of shyness. Many, if not all, people can be shy at times. This is common when, say, we're invited to a party where we don't know anyone but the host. Even if we aren't insecure, we may feel uncomfortable with the idea of introducing ourselves to strangers. This initial shyness, though, usually ebbs as we get comfortable in a new social setting. We relax and end up having a good time. For those with a social phobia, the mere thought of going to any party, much less one with strangers, will be so overwhelming that it causes panic. They would do anything to avoid going to a party where they don't know anyone! Shyness is not a milder version of the same reaction; it's like the difference between cautiously entering a busy freeway and being too afraid to drive. A social phobia feels like an impassable roadblock that stops you dead in your tracks.

Social anxiety disorder has several main causes; it may be learned, inherited, or the result of biology. People with social phobias have good threat detectors. Too good, in fact: They see danger when there is nothing to fear. People with social phobias often feel like total losers, since they find themselves unable to do the sorts of things, like go to parties, that everyone else enjoys easily.

Many people with social phobias can trace their anxieties to a specific humiliating experience: peeing their pants in class or losing a softball game by striking out, for example. Those memories can burn themselves into the brain, so that when people are placed in similar situations, all they can hear are the jeers and laughter of others. Nobody wants to repeat those awful experiences, so they tend to avoid situations that will put them at risk for ridicule.

In addition, social anxiety disorder tends to run in families. We inherit eye, skin, and hair color from our parents—as well as the tendency to have social phobias. If someone in a person's immediate family has a social anxiety disorder, that person is two to three times more likely to suffer from it compared with someone who doesn't have that family connection. Charles Darwin noticed this all the way back in 1872, when he quoted a physician who said, "Even peculiarities in blushing seem to be inherited."

Recently, scientists have found that people with social anxiety seem to be genetically programmed to be more anxious. They may have an imbalance of certain brain chemicals or over-achieving amygdalae—the parts of the brain that process fear. The brains of people with social phobias respond much more strongly to pictures of angry or frowning faces than those of people with no social anxiety. They're hypersensitive to negative feedback from other people.

Social anxiety is also something that people learn from their parents. If a parent obsesses over what other people think of themselves or their family, that parent may have an anxiety disorder—and their children may be on the road to developing their own. Overprotective parents may unintentionally teach their kids to be afraid of social situations, such as whether people are going to laugh at their new glasses.

FAMOUS PHOBICS

Former football player Ricky Williams had always considered himself shy, but things got pretty tough when the Heisman Trophy winner found himself in the spotlight as a running back for the New Orleans Saints. He became known for doing press interviews with his helmet on, complete with dark visor. If he had to go to the supermarket to buy something, he'd run from one aisle to another, trying to avoid fans who might recognize him. He once said, "I felt extremely isolated from my friends and family because I couldn't explain to them what I was feeling."

A friend urged Williams to see a therapist, and he was diagnosed with social anxiety disorder. He improved greatly after therapy, and he started taking medications. Now he is a spokesperson for the disorder.

Williams's story is a familiar one in the world of sports. People who are already prone to anxiety can become overwhelmed with the pressure to perform well. Baseball players Zack Greinke and Khalil Greene and Olympic swimmer Susie O'Neill are among the sports figures who have had public struggles with social anxiety.

OVERCOMING THE FEAR

Social anxiety disorder is an extremely crippling phobia. With many of the phobias in this book, it can be pretty easy to avoid what's feared, such as sharks, snakes, dolls, beards, and so on. You can manage your life successfully without necessarily overcoming the fear. But avoiding people is a different story. Many people with social anxieties live with their disorders for decades before seeking help—if they ever do. The very act of reaching out to someone for help can itself be a source of panic. Not only is one's life filled with constant worry about what other people think, but social phobias can keep people from getting necessary treatment. This can make people vulnerable to other problems, like depression and alcohol and drug abuse.

Like other anxiety disorders, social phobias can be effectively treated. While the techniques described in "Overcoming the Fear" (page 199) can help, it's important to also work with a professional therapist. Therapists can help you change the thought patterns that make you anxious and practice new behaviors. Sometimes, but not always, they will prescribe medications that reduce anxiety.

SCARE QUOTES

"Shyness has a strange element of narcissism, a belief that how we look, how we perform, is truly important to other people."
—Writer André Dubus

"Nobody realizes that some people expend tremendous energy merely to be normal."
—Albert Camus

"And the day came when the risk to remain tight in a bud was more painful than the risk it took to blossom."
—Writer Anaïs Nin

"I understand that a lot of people, especially men, look up to me because of my profession, so I have a chance to reach out to people and let them know what I've been through and how treatment has made my life so much better. If my story can help even one person to seek help, it will feel as though I've scored the game-winning touchdown."
—Football player Ricky Williams

SOMNIPHOBIA

FEAR OF SLEEP

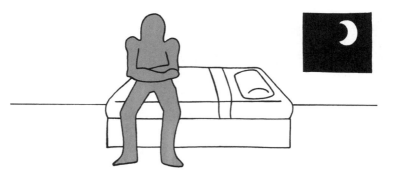

S leep is as necessary for survival as eating and drinking. It's not just a matter of feeling cranky when we don't get enough sleep—although there's that—but of staying healthy. Extreme, long-term sleep deprivation can even be deadly. But many people with anxiety disorders fear sleep for a variety of reasons.

Indeed, somniphobia—the term is from the Latin word *somnus*, meaning "sleep," and the fear is also known as hypnophobia—is related to a host of other fears: fear of sleepwalking, fear of sleep talking, fear of nightmares or night terrors, and even fear of death (thanatophobia, page 178).

In the most basic terms, if you're anxious or stressed, it's harder to sleep, and you're more likely to be plagued by nightmares. Whether you dream about drowning or being chased by bad guys, nightmares are by definition scary, and it's hard to get back to sleep once you've had one. Some people wake up in the middle of the night feeling completely panicked even without remembering a nightmare. Nightmares and sleep panics happen to most people occasionally. It's impossible to live a stress-free life. But people who are plagued by them on a regular basis are more likely to fear falling asleep—and sleep deprivation can lead to even more anxiety. It's a vicious cycle!

Less common, but truly freaky, is something called sleep paralysis. Imagine waking up at night only to find that you can't move a muscle. You sense an evil presence hovering just beyond your line of vision or even sitting on your chest, crushing the breath out of your lungs. This terrifying experience is sleep paralysis, and it can last anywhere from a few minutes to an hour. Many cultures have imagined a variety of supernatural explanations: that, say, a hag, witch, demon, or the spirit of a dead person, settles on top of the helpless victim.

Sleep paralysis happens when our brain wakes up from sleep—usually during a dreaming state—but our muscles are still paralyzed. It is normal for our muscles to relax to the point of paralysis when we are dreaming, probably to prevent us from acting out our dreams. About 6 percent of people experience sleep paralysis, but maybe only once or a few times in a lifetime. Yet some people experience it over and over again—and it makes a potent reason to fear sleep!

Then, some people are prone to talking in their sleep and fear what they might say or reveal. Usually sleep talkers just mumble gibberish, but it can be unnerving to imagine ourselves talking when we aren't conscious of it or in control of what we're saying.

Sleepwalking can also provide a good reason to fear sleep. Most of the time, a sleepwalker does something benign, and the only thing that's potentially troubling is the fact that sleepwalking happened. But sleepwalkers have also been known to try to jump out a window or drive a car, and these scenarios are obviously dangerous for the sleepwalker—and sometimes for others.

For some, somniphobia is related to that most elemental of all fears: the fear of death. Death is called the "big sleep" for a reason, since they can be unsettlingly similar states: you are no longer aware of your surroundings, you are vulnerable, and you are no longer in control of your situation. This is an especially common fear of children once they grasp an understanding of death. The euphemisms we sometimes use for death don't help: what's a child to think when parents put a beloved family dog "to sleep," or when they say the dog "didn't wake up," or that a grandparent "died peacefully in her sleep"? These expressions are meant to be comforting, but they may become the opposite when the child's own bedtime rolls around.

FAMOUS PHOBICS

British singer Leona Lewis is a sleepwalker. She doesn't lose any sleep over it, though; she makes sure that the windows to her balcony are locked so that she can't climb out and fall.

Comedian Mike Birbiglia has not only admitted to having some dangerous sleepwalking experiences, he's written, directed, and starred in a 2012 film based on them, *Sleepwalk with Me*.

OVERCOMING THE FEAR

If sleep problems are caused by anxiety and stress, some of the relaxation techniques described in "Overcoming the Fear" (page 199) can often help. Prime your body for a good night's sleep by taking a warm bath, drinking warm milk, or listening to some calming music. If you're prone to nightmares, don't eat any late-night snacks: They signal your brain to be more active. Don't drink coffee or other caffeinated drinks in the four or five hours before bedtime. Exercise regularly—but not too close to bed-time. Finally, avoid sitting in front of a lighted computer screen right before bedtime: That bright light sends the wrong signals to your brain. If nothing helps and you are still scared to sleep, talk to a therapist who specializes in sleep disorders.

SCARE QUOTES

"Oh, the terrible struggle that I have had against sleep so often of late; the pain of the sleeplessness, or the pain of the fear of sleep, and with such unknown horror as it has for me! How blessed are some people, whose lives have no fears, no dreads; to whom sleep is a blessing that comes nightly, and brings nothing but sweet dreams."
—Bram Stoker, *Dracula*

"Since his majesty went into the field, I have seen her rise from her bed, throw her night-gown upon her, unlock her closet, take forth paper, fold it, write upon't, read it, afterwards seal it, and again return to bed; yet all this while in a most fast sleep."
—Shakespeare, *Macbeth*, in which a maid describes Lady Macbeth's sleepwalking

"I'm afraid to sleep. It's a form of death."
—Edith Piaf, French singer

SPECTROPHOBIA

FEAR OF MIRRORS

Mirrors as objects don't hold the same mystical powers that they once seemed to, and so fear of mirrors is not very prevalent anymore. When this fear is mentioned today, it more often refers to a fear of one's own reflection. Indeed, in today's image-obsessed society, some people really are afraid to look in mirrors because they fear they don't meet some standard of beauty. Like the evil queen in the Snow White fairy tale, they are afraid mirrors will turn on them and tell them they are no longer pretty.

The term *spectrophobia* derives from the Latin word *spectrum*, for "ghost." The phobia is also known as catoptrophobia (the term is from the Greek word *katoptron,* for "mirror"), while the related phobia of fear of your own reflection is sometimes called eisoptrophobia—the name is a combination of the Greek words *eis*, "into," and *optikos,* "vision."

The roots of all these mirror phobias can be traced back to ancient fears and superstitions. Back when mirrors were just pools of still water or shiny pieces of obsidian, people believed that their reflections were actually their souls looking back at them. (This is why vampires have no reflections—they have no souls!) A broken reflection was an ominous sign, and so a broken mirror came to portend bad luck.

THE BLOODY MARY GAME

A popular scary slumber party game called Bloody Mary helps illustrate the enduring power of mirrors to freak people out. (Those with spectrophobia might want to stop reading now!)

The game goes something like this: Begin in a darkened room that contains a mirror and is lit by a single candle. All the participants prick their fingers while repeating "I believe in Bloody Mary" ten times. Then each person stands before the mirror, staring into it and chanting "Bloody Mary" thirteen times. This ritual is supposed to cause the gruesome ghost of Bloody Mary to appear, as if reaching through the mirror to scratch your face. At this point, it's important to scream and run hysterically from the room.

Depending on what part of the country you are from, "Bloody Mary" refers to several historical or legendary women. One Bloody Mary legend says that she lived in Massachusetts in the seventeenth century; she was charged with witchcraft, tortured, and hanged. In other versions, she was either murdered or killed in a tragic car accident.

Perhaps obviously, this party game turns on an optical illusion, and it may help explain why mirrors are used in divination. When people stare into a dimly lit mirror for up to ten minutes, they start to see some crazy things. In one experiment, participants reported seeing their own faces, but hideously deformed; the faces of their parents, with some features changed; or the face of a stranger or an animal. Nearly half of the people in the study saw some sort of monstrous being. Apparently our brains get tired of staring at the same thing after a while and start to make freaky stuff up. And if you're primed to see Bloody Mary . . .

The association of mirrors with the soul led to the custom, popular in Victorian times, of covering all the mirrors while a corpse was in the house. They believed that anybody who saw their reflection in the mirror of a house where someone just died was likely to die soon. A covered mirror would also ensure that the soul of the departed would be forever trapped behind the glass. The Jewish practice of covering mirrors in a house of mourning does not appear to be related to these superstitions; in Hebrew tradition, mourners are supposed to focus on the loved one rather than on themselves.

MEMORABLE MIRRORS IN MYTH AND LITERATURE

In Greek mythology, Narcissus was the gorgeous son of a river god and a nymph. He fell in love with his reflection in a pool of water, not realizing it was merely his own image. It's not recorded in history, but he may have been the original dumb jock. Unable to pull himself away from his beautiful image, he died of sorrow because he realized he couldn't have the object of his desire. His name is the root of the word *narcissism*. Indeed, in stories, falling in love with one's own reflection nearly always leads to bad consequences; just ask Snow White's evil queen, who famously kept asking, "Mirror, mirror, on the wall. Who's the fairest of them all?" Eventually, she didn't like the answer.

In J. K. Rowling's book *Harry Potter and the Sorcerer's Stone*, this idea is given an interesting twist. The "Mirror of Erised" also contains a danger for those who become entranced with it, but of a different sort. As its translated inscription reads, "I show not your face but your heart's desire." Harry, of course, sees his dead parents, and he finds it nearly impossible to look away.

In Lewis Carroll's book *Through the Looking-Glass*, which is the sequel to *Alice in Wonderland*, Alice is able to step through a mirror into an alternate world. Many stories use this device, which merely treats as real what all mirrors seem to show: that there is a world inside them.

In J. R. R. Tolkien's *Lord of the Rings* trilogy, the elven Lady Galadriel has a mirror—actually, a silver basin of water—with some pretty amazing powers of divination. In Peter Jackson's movie *The Lord of the Rings: The Fellowship of the Ring*, Galadriel tells Frodo, "The mirror shows many things. Things that were. Things that are. And some things that have not yet come to pass." The tricky part is figuring out which is which.

From the reflection-soul connection, it's just a hop, skip, and a jump to the idea that mirrors could be used to communicate with other worlds. In the seventeenth and eighteenth centuries, the practice of mirror divination, or catoptromancy (now, *there's* a good word), became common. One of the most famous seers was Nostradamus, who used a mirror or sometimes a bowl of water to peer into the future, making a bunch of predictions that some people think have come, and are coming, true. At any rate, mirror divination, or scrying, has come to be associated with witchcraft.

FAMOUS PHOBICS

Actress Pamela Anderson is a famous spectrophobe. She has said, "I have this phobia: I don't like mirrors. And I don't watch myself on television. If anything comes on, I make them shut it off, or I leave the room."

SWINOPHOBIA

FEAR OF PIGS

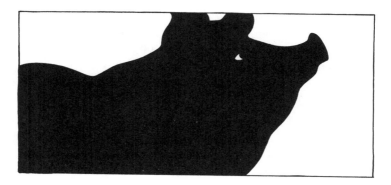

If the very thought of piggies makes you want to go "wee-wee-wee all the way home," then you may have swinophobia (the name derives from the Old English word *swin*, for "pig" or "hog"). This is not a very common phobia, but it does exist.

People who have never seen a real, full-size pig up close may wonder what there is to be afraid of. Almost invariably, pigs in popular culture are cute, cuddly, smart, and talkative. For instance, there is the adorable pig in the 1995 movie *Babe,* who just wants to be a sheepdog. Wilbur, in E. B. White's classic book *Charlotte's Web,* is "Terrific, Radiant, Humble." The Muppet character Miss Piggy is far from humble, but she is certainly radiant. And then, of course, Ian Falconer's children's-book heroine Olivia, who "is good at lots of things," and Winnie-the-Pooh's friend Piglet couldn't be more lovable.

Real-life pigs? They can actually be pretty frightening. Adult pigs usually weigh in at 250 to 300 pounds, and they can reach up to 1,000 pounds. On sheer bulk alone, they can appear intimidating. But they truly are very smart, they grunt and squeal and shake their flappy ears, and if they are not kept in a clean environment, they can smell pretty rank.

Plus, in some parts of the country, feral pigs (formerly domesticated pigs that have escaped and now roam wild) are a real problem. They tear up and destroy ecosystems and farmland, kill pets and smaller animals, and aggressively threaten humans with their fearsome tusks.

This is enough for some people to blindly fear all pigs. But swinophobia can also be triggered by a frightening experience early in life. Though it may in fact have been a harmless encounter, a negative impression made early on can last a long time. That said, most people who want to avoid pigs find this relatively easy to do, and the phobia responds well to the techniques described in "Overcoming the Fear" (page 199).

On a side note, many Jews and Muslims avoid eating pork for religious reasons. While they are sometimes described as "swinophobes," that's not really accurate. They don't necessarily fear pigs; they simply abstain from eating them as a matter of custom.

FAMOUS PHOBICS

When a pig escaped on the set of *Kingdom of Heaven,* actor Orlando Bloom reportedly fled in terror.

Bloom may be the only famous person who's come clean about his fear of pigs, but the cast of the reality-TV show *American Hoggers* know that he's not alone. The show chronicles the lives of the legendary Campbell family, known for hunting and killing the feral pigs that have been terrorizing Texas. As they say on the show, "Anything that weighs up to 400 pounds, runs at 30 miles per hour and eats its own young is no joke."

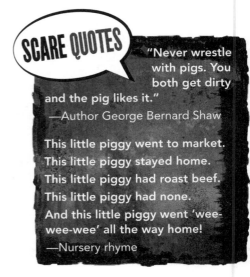

SCARE QUOTES

"Never wrestle with pigs. You both get dirty and the pig likes it."
—Author George Bernard Shaw

This little piggy went to market.
This little piggy stayed home.
This little piggy had roast beef.
This little piggy had none.
And this little piggy went 'wee-wee-wee' all the way home!
—Nursery rhyme

TAPHOPHOBIA

There are few things more terrifying than the idea of being buried alive, and if this were still the Victorian era, taphophobia (the term is from the Greek *taphos*, meaning "grave" or "tomb") would not be uncommon. Edgar Allen Poe seems to have been obsessed with it, and several other well-known artists feared the possibility. Today, it's almost never seen, though taphophobia sometimes accompanies a host of related fears, such as coimetrophobia (fear of cemeteries), claustrophobia (fear of enclosed spaces, page 57), fear of tombstones (placophobia), and fear of death (thanatophobia, page 178).

In Poe's horror story "The Premature Burial," the narrator squeamishly warns his readers, "There are certain themes of which the interest is all-absorbing, but which are too entirely horrible for the purposes of legitimate fiction." Poe, however, had no trouble at all pondering premature burial in his fiction. In addition to "The Premature Burial," there is "The Cask of Amontillado," in which poor Fortunato is walled into a niche in his wine cellar by his friend Montresor. (Really, with friends like that . . .) And in one of Poe's most famous tales, "The Fall of the House of Usher," Roderick Usher realizes that he has unfortunately entombed his sister, who was ill but most emphatically not dead.

Somehow, she escapes and appears, bloody and emaciated, to her brother, who dies of sheer terror. (Moral: Do not mess with your sister.)

In the nineteenth century, the fear of being buried alive wasn't entirely without cause. For centuries, the hallmark of death was when the heart stopped beating. The only problem was that if the heartbeat was very faint, it could be very difficult for a doctor to hear it. The stethoscope wasn't invented until the middle of the nineteenth century, and even then it wasn't very good. Stories of premature burial abounded, including one in which an undertaker's servant dug up a wealthy woman who had been buried with an expensive ring. As he opened her coffin, she sat up and the grave robber ran away. According to the story, she walked to her house and rang the doorbell.

Not surprisingly, people devised all sorts of methods for determining whether the deceased was actually dead. They included cutting the soles of the feet, pinching nipples, or playing loud music—presumably, all methods that would wake a living person. But the gold standard for determining death was just to wait a few days. If the body began to decompose, it was a safe bet that burial was necessary.

Given this grim history, taphophobia was not always an irrational fear. But rest assured (so to speak). Modern medical

SECURITY COFFINS

In the late eighteenth and early nineteenth centuries, fear of premature burial created a market for something new: the security coffin. Some of the first recorded safety coffins had air tubes to provide a supply of fresh air or strings connected to bells above ground that the recently deceased could ring should they find themselves not deceased. Some even had shovels, in case the buried wretch should have the energy to dig out.

Rumors that the phrases "saved by the bell" and "dead ringer" originated with security coffins are, unfortunately, untrue. "Saved by the bell" is a boxing term dating from the 1930s. "Dead ringer" came from horse racing, in which a fast horse would be swapped with a similar-looking nag.

procedures for determining death, as well as the increasingly common practices of embalming and cremation, make it practically impossible for anyone today to be buried alive.

FAMOUS PHOBICS

Whether they were truly taphophobic or just realists, several famous folks were very concerned about premature burial and went to great lengths to ensure that they were good and dead before they were put into the ground.

On his deathbed, George Washington said, "I am just going. Have me decently buried; and do not let my body be put into the Vault in less than three days after I am dead."

Hans Christian Andersen lived in mortal fear of being buried alive. He distrusted foreign doctors; when he traveled, he always carried with him a card that read, "I am not really dead." Shortly before his death in 1875, he asked a friend to make sure his arteries were severed before he was buried.

SCARE QUOTES

"The movement of the jaws, in this effort to cry aloud, showed me that they were bound up, as is usual with the dead. I felt, too, that I lay upon some hard substance; and by something similar my sides were, also, closely compressed. So far, I had not ventured to stir any of my limbs—but now I violently threw up my arms, which had been lying at length, with the wrists crossed. They struck a solid wooden substance, which extended above my person at an elevation of not more than six inches from my face. I could no longer doubt that I reposed within a coffin at last."

—Edgar Allen Poe, *The Premature Burial*

"The earth is suffocating. . . . Swear to make them cut me open, so that I won't be buried alive."

—Composer Frédéric Chopin's last words

THANATOPHOBIA

FEAR OF DEATH

In a way, avoiding death is one of the main purposes of life. Fail in this, and we have little else to worry about. Out of all human fears, it's probably the most universal. But when the fear of dying overwhelms us and becomes thanatophobia, we can lose the ability to really live. As a phobia, thanatophobia (*thanatos* is the Greek term for the demonic personification of death) is behind or accompanies a number of other phobias, such as fears of diseases or accidents and fear of darkness, falling, hospitals, sleep, heights, and more.

Thanatophobia is also only the most important of a host of death-related fears, such as fear of corpses (necrophobia), fear of ghosts (phasmophobia or daemonophobia), fear of tombstones (placophobia), fear of cemeteries (coimetrophobia), fear of zombies (kinemortophobia), and fear of being buried alive (taphophobia, page 175).

In general in the United States, death is regarded by many as a taboo subject. People often speak of it in euphemisms. Instead of saying that someone has died, people say they have "passed," are "no longer with us," or have gone to their "eternal rest." When pets are euthanized, they are "put to sleep." In these

FAMOUS EPITAPHS

Not everyone fears their own death. Or, if they do, they come to accept this inevitability with grace and good humor. At least, that's the impression we get from these memorable, and real, gravestone epitaphs!

"That's all, folks."

—Mel Blanc (1908–1989). Blanc was the voice actor behind Bugs Bunny, Porky Pig, Daffy Duck, Tweety Bird, Yosemite Sam, Foghorn Leghorn, and many others.

"I am ready to meet my Maker. Whether my Maker is prepared for the great ordeal of meeting me is another matter."

—Winston Churchill (1874–1965)

"I told you I was ill."

—Spike Milligan (1918–2002), an English-Irish comedian, writer, and actor. The actual inscription is in Gaelic because the local church thought that the epitaph was undignified.

"Excuse my dust."

—Dorothy Parker (1893–1967), an American author and humorist. In her will, Parker left her estate to Martin Luther King, whom she admired but had never met. She was cremated, and her ashes were stored in a file cabinet until being buried outside the headquarters of the National Association for the Advancement of Colored People, in Baltimore, Maryland.

"Quote the Raven: 'Nevermore.'"

—Edgar Allen Poe (1809–1849). Poe's epitaph is, of course, from his most famous poem, "The Raven."

"Good frend for Jesus sake forebeare, To digg the dust enclosed heare; Bleste be the man that spares these stones, And curst be he that moves my bones."

William Shakespeare (ca. 1564–1616). Digging up the bones of the dead was common in Shakespeare's day; he wanted to make sure that his stayed put.

ways, as a culture, we indicate that we are afraid of death. For some, this is fear of the unknown—and death is the ultimate unknown. Some fear the process of dying, and some fear leaving the people they love. Those who believe in a hereafter may indeed worry about where they will end up. But for anyone, contemplating death often  means contemplating the summary of one's life, which may bring up a host of negative feelings: fears, doubts, disappointments, judgments, and regrets.

All of this means that thanatophobia is fairly common, though it is not always experienced as an extreme fear in and of itself. Thankfully, it is often effectively treated with the help of a professional therapist. While many phobias are related to the fear of death, thanatophobia isn't any more difficult to treat than others, and addressing it directly is often a good way to help resolve other, more object- or situation-specific phobias.

Paradoxically, an excessive fear of death may actually hasten our demise. Scientists have shown that people with phobic anxieties such as the fear of crowded places, heights, or going outside—all anxieties that are often associated with thanatophobia—are at higher risk for fatal heart disease than those with fewer or no anxieties. And, yes, it is even possible, though rare, to be scared to death. When we are frightened and have a panic attack, our fight-or-flight nervous system releases adrenaline and other stress hormones that prepare the body for action. Most of the time, we take this adrenaline rush in stride; in fact, many of us love roller coasters just to get that feeling of terror! But occasionally, those stress hormones can cause fatal heart attacks.

FAMOUS PHOBICS

Actress Sarah Michelle Gellar, who played Buffy in the TV series *Buffy the Vampire Slayer,* has admitted to being phobic about cemeteries and the thought of being buried alive. In one episode, her character Buffy had to dig her way out of her own grave. "It was horrible," Gellar said. "It's really hard to be a vampire slayer if you're scared of cemeteries."

Some people are more notable for the courage with which they face death than for their fear of death. In 2007, forty-six-year-old computer science professor Randy Pausch gave a lecture called "Really Achieving Your Childhood Dreams." Despite his youthful and energetic appearance, he told the audience that he had terminal cancer. Rather than talk about his impending death, he gave an inspirational (and at times even funny) lecture about the lessons he'd learned about living. His lecture went viral on YouTube and was turned into a bestselling book titled *The Last Lecture*.

SCARE QUOTES

"For to fear death, gentlemen, is nothing else than to think one is wise when one is not; for it is thinking one knows what one does not know. For no one knows whether death be not even the greatest of all blessings to man, but they fear it as if they knew that it is the greatest of evils."

—Socrates, quoted by Plato in *The Apology*

"The fear of death follows from the fear of life. A man who lives fully is prepared to die at any time."

—Mark Twain

"I'm not afraid of dying; I just don't want to be there when it happens."

—Woody Allen

TOPOPHOBIA

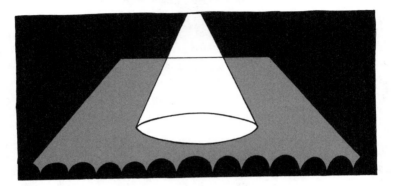

Performance anxiety, stage fright, fear of speaking in public—they're all related forms of social anxiety that fall under the umbrella of topophobia (the term is from the Greek word *topos*, meaning "place"). If the thought of appearing onstage or behind a podium and talking, singing, acting, or otherwise performing in front of an audience makes you break out in a cold sweat, you have a lot of company. Some claim that the fear of public speaking—which is also called glossophobia, after the Greek word *glōssa,* for "tongue"—is the number one fear in the country: As many as three out of four people feel anxious about it. Of course, most of those people don't have a true phobia. Their fear doesn't stop them from performing in public, and despite their anxiety, they manage to get their acts together and carry on. But still, for many people—one study estimates as many as 40 percent—their fear of performing causes real and ongoing problems in school, at work, and in social settings.

Experience doesn't matter, either. We might think it natural that someone who'd never performed before, or who did it only occasionally, would be afraid. But debilitating stage fright affects even accomplished musicians, actors, and politicians—anybody whose job requires them to perform.

Stage fright is all about the fear of making a mistake or looking stupid or uncertain in front of others. It's normal to feel nervous when getting up in front of a crowd. In fact, many performers regard a little adrenaline as helpful for a performance or for focusing your thoughts during a presentation. That's not what we're talking about here. What topophobia refers to is the onset of panicky, fight-or-flight symptoms: a dry mouth, pounding heart, trembling, sweating, blushing, and nausea.

With mild performance anxiety, people often find that once they get started, they forget their nervousness and relax into the performance or speech. People in the grip of topophobia experience the opposite: They tend to get more and more nervous as they go. They focus on their trembling hands or sweaty armpits instead of the performance. Once topophobia takes hold, people become hypersensitive to the audience's reaction and any signs they don't like what they see: *Did someone just yawn? Oh, no, I'm boring! Is someone texting? They're probably tweeting about how crappy I am.*

Some people develop topophobia before they've ever performed even once. However, it's much more common for it to arise after a bad performance or experience onstage. Then, the fear of it happening again is what stops people. Even the most accomplished artists and celebrities can be stricken by it—just ask Barbra Streisand!

FAMOUS PHOBICS

Sir Laurence Olivier, one of the greatest actors of the twentieth century, developed stage fright midway through his career. It got so bad that he had to be pushed out onto the stage during every performance.

Barbra Streisand developed stage fright in 1967 when she forgot the lyrics to a song while performing in front of 135,000 people at a free concert in Central Park. She avoided live performances for nearly three decades after that.

Singer Carly Simon has struggled with stage fright throughout her career. She rarely performs live, explaining that while most

183

performers feel butterflies before a show, she gets "large bats." One time, early in her career, Simon was performing on a small stage when she looked out into the audience and saw her musical hero, Odetta. She fainted and woke up lying on the floor, Odetta fanning her with a menu.

OVERCOMING THE FEAR

Fortunately, there are effective ways to overcome performance anxiety and stage fright. One of the most common is cognitive behavioral therapy (see "Overcoming the Fear," page 199). Another great and simple method is plain-old practice: You can find groups that teach performance techniques and then allow you to rehearse them in front of a few friendly faces. Or, gather a few of your own friends and do this. Therapists also sometimes prescribe medications to help professional performers tame the jitters. Of course, some performers are legendary for turning to drugs and alcohol to manage their stage fright, but this is not a good idea!

SCARE QUOTES

"According to most studies, people's number one fear is public speaking. Number two is death. Death is number two. Does that sound right? This means, to the average person, if you go to a funeral, you're better off in the casket than doing the eulogy."
—Comedian Jerry Seinfeld

"There are only two types of speakers in the world. 1. The nervous and 2. Liars."
—Mark Twain

"It's amazing. You can look out front of a big crowd—let's say twenty thousand people in the auditorium—but I'll find the one in front who doesn't clap."
—Barbra Streisand, on why she likes to perform only in darkened auditoriums

TRISKAIDEKAPHOBIA

FEAR OF THIRTEEN

FRI.　OCT.
1 3

Whether it's considered just a superstition or a true phobia, triskaidekaphobia certainly leads to some interesting behavior. For centuries, the number 13 has been considered unlucky, and many people go to great lengths to avoid any association with it.

For instance, elevator experts estimate that as many as 85 percent of high-rise buildings in the world don't have a thirteenth floor: the buttons simply skip from 12 to 14. However, as firefighters point out, pretending that there is no thirteenth floor could bring its own very bad luck: if they are called to put out a fire on the fourteenth floor—but it's actually the thirteenth floor—and firefighters count floors from the outside, they may well direct their fire hoses at the wrong floor!

In many cities, there are no house or streets numbered 13. Some airports don't have Gate 13. Many people, especially in Europe, consider it unlucky to have thirteen guests at a dinner party. In France, superstitious dinner hosts can hire a professional fourteenth guest!

Triskaidekaphobia's wonderfully alliterative name comes from combining three Greek words: *tris*, meaning "three"; *kai*, meaning "and"; and *deka*, meaning "ten." In the United States, perhaps an even more common phobia is friggatriskaidekaphobia, or fear of Friday the 13th. The Norse gave us their fear of the number 13, and the name of the Norse goddess Frigga gave us the word Friday, so it makes sense to combine them. However, people who prefer Greek roots call this paraskevidekatriaphobia—*paraskevi* is the Greek word for "Friday," and *dekatreis* means "thirteen."

Friggatriskaidekaphobia is probably the most common superstition in the United States; according to researchers, it affects 17 to 21 million people. Businesses lose an estimated $800 to $900 million on any given Friday the 13th because people call in sick to work, postpone travel, or delay making major purchases.

As was mentioned, fear of the number 13 may be traced back to Norse mythology. According to the Vikings, twelve gods were having a fabulous dinner party in Valhalla, their version of heaven. The most beloved of these gods was Balder, the god of truth and light. He was so beloved, in fact, that everything in the nine worlds—from weapons to disease and creatures of every sort—pledged not to harm Balder.

The trickster god Loki crashed the party, disguised as an old woman. He learned

THE THIRTEEN CLUB

William Fowler decided that he'd had enough of this nonsense about how the number 13 was unlucky. After all, the Civil War veteran had fought in thirteen major battles. He retired from combat on August 13, 1863, and bought a house on the thirteenth of the month. And so, on Friday, January 13, 1882, at thirteen minutes past the hour, Fowler and twelve other men sat down to dinner. Over the years, members of the club violated every superstition they could think of: they walked under ladders to get to the dinner table, spilled salt without throwing some over their shoulders, broke mirrors, and placed open umbrellas around the dining room.

Five US presidents joined the club: Chester A. Arthur, Grover Cleveland, Benjamin Harrison, William McKinley, and Theodore Roosevelt.

that there was one tiny thing that had not made the pledge: mistletoe. He tricked Balder's blind brother, Hod, into shooting Balder with an arrow made from a branch of mistletoe. The beautiful Balder died, and Loki—the unlucky thirteenth member of the dinner party—fled.

The ancient Persians believed that there were twelve astrological ages, each lasting a thousand years; at the end of the twelve ages, the earth and sky would collapse in chaos. Christian legend has it that Judas, the disciple who betrayed Jesus, was the thirteenth person to sit at the table.

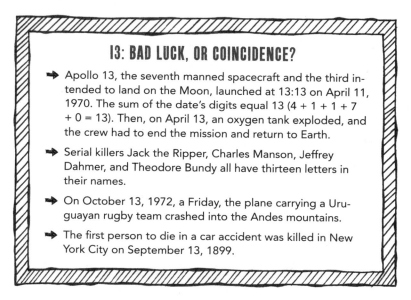

13: BAD LUCK, OR COINCIDENCE?

➡ Apollo 13, the seventh manned spacecraft and the third intended to land on the Moon, launched at 13:13 on April 11, 1970. The sum of the date's digits equal 13 (4 + 1 + 1 + 7 + 0 = 13). Then, on April 13, an oxygen tank exploded, and the crew had to end the mission and return to Earth.

➡ Serial killers Jack the Ripper, Charles Manson, Jeffrey Dahmer, and Theodore Bundy all have thirteen letters in their names.

➡ On October 13, 1972, a Friday, the plane carrying a Uruguayan rugby team crashed into the Andes mountains.

➡ The first person to die in a car accident was killed in New York City on September 13, 1899.

The fear of Friday the 13th seems to be a more recent superstition. Some considered Friday unlucky because that was the day Jesus was crucified. Some time around 1800, people began to get the idea that it was bad luck to start a journey, get married, or start a new job on a Friday. Combine the two—Friday and 13—and you've got a toxic combination of bad juju.

Why do we persist in believing these superstitions? One reason may be that our brains are good at making associations. If something bad happens to you on Friday the 13th, the coincidence will probably stick with you. You won't remember all of the uneventful Friday the 13th days. One study published in the *British Medical Journal* found that people are more likely to be involved in a car accident on a Friday the 13th than on other Fridays. People who are anxious, they reasoned, are simply more prone to make mistakes. In other words, friggetriskaidekaphobics can bring about their own bad luck. Ouch!

FAMOUS PHOBICS

President Franklin D. Roosevelt would not travel on the thirteenth day of any month, and he would avoid dinners where there would be thirteen guests. Herbert Hoover was also known to be triskaidekaphobic; when he was running for president, a Democratic senator tried to rattle Hoover by asking him to answer thirteen questions about what he would do if elected. (Herbert won, anyway.)

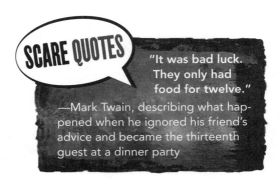

SCARE QUOTES

"It was bad luck. They only had food for twelve."

—Mark Twain, describing what happened when he ignored his friend's advice and became the thirteenth guest at a dinner party

TRYPANOPHOBIA

FEAR OF NEEDLES

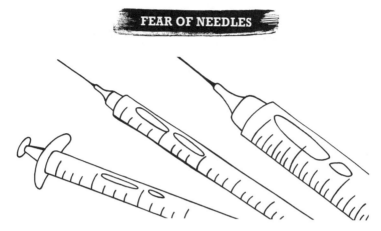

For about 10 percent of Americans, the scariest thing in the doctor's office is the needle. In fact, the number of people with trypanophobia (named for the Greek word *trypano*, meaning "borer") may be even higher, since people with a serious fear of needles tend to avoid going to the doctor altogether. People with needle phobias frequently experience panic attacks, lightheadedness, or fainting when they're around needles. The fear of needles prevents many people from getting needed vaccinations, blood tests, or other medical care, so it's a serious issue. Related needle phobias include belonephobia (fear of sewing-type needles and pins) and aichmophobia (fear of sharp, pointy things).

The most common type of trypanophobia is actually an inherited physical reflex in response to needles. About half of all trypano-phobes have this reflex, and it definitely runs in families. When they see or even think about injections, their heart rate and blood pressure spike and then immediately plunge. When this happens, trypanophobes may hear a ringing in their ears, see stars, and feel dizzy. They may even find themselves on the floor, passed out. Many people with this condition say they don't fear the needle as much as they do the prospect of keeling over in the doctor's office; in this way, it's similar to other panic disorders, like phobophobia (page 139) and agoraphobia (page 26), and it's very similar to hemophobia, or the fear of blood (page 85). A few people have actually died after having this reaction, making trypanophobia one of the few phobias that actually *can* kill you. There may be an evolutionary reason why some people have this response: It's a good idea to avoid stab wounds!

Not everyone with trypanophobia has inherited this reflex. Some fear needles because of a traumatic past experience: either when they had an injection or when they watched someone else get a shot. If someone, as a little kid, was once forcibly held down to get their shots, the fear may involve being controlled or restrained. Finally, some people simply experience pain more acutely than the rest of us. This is true for about 10 percent of those with trypanophobia. For them, the dreaded promise "Now, this won't hurt a bit" is just one big fat lie.

FAMOUS PHOBICS

Heavyweight boxer Sonny Liston had a bad-boy reputation, even in the rough-and-tumble world of boxing. Tough as he was, Liston was deathly afraid of needles. After winning the heavy-weight title, he refused to go on an exhibition tour in Europe when he found out he would have to get shots to travel over-seas. His well-known fear of needles led many of his friends to believe that Sonny Liston had in fact been murdered when he was found with needle tracks in his arms, dead of an apparent heroin overdose.

Late-night talk show host Conan O'Brian refuses to get a flu shot, citing his fear of needles.

Martial arts movie star Jackie Chan has performed most of his own dangerous stunts, but he has a real needle phobia. Never-theless, he made a video of himself giving blood. The star, who is known for his generosity, wanted to show how important it is to help others in need.

OVERCOMING THE FEAR

If you know that you're a fainter when it
comes to needles, tell the doctor or nurse. If
you need an injection or blood test, they will
make sure you lie down or sit in a reclining
chair. This is often enough to prevent fainting,
and it means no harm will result if you do.

Also, when you must get a shot, try the deep breathing
and relaxation exercises described in "Overcoming the
Fear" (page 199). Then, practice the art of distraction. Bring
your MP3 player and listen to some music, or close your eyes
and imagine lying on a warm beach far, far away. Some physi-
cians and nurses swear by the cough trick. Before the injection,
do a warm up cough, and then cough again when it comes time
for the shot. If pain sensitivity is the issue, then a numbing
cream or spray may be useful. However, if these techniques don't
help, or especially if you have a chronic disease like diabetes
that requires frequent injections, consider seeing a therapist to
help work through your fear. As a last resort, some doctors may
prescribe antianxiety medications.

SCARE QUOTES

"When the daughter of the king turns
fifteen, she will prick her finger on a
spindle and fall down dead."

—The curse of the thirteenth wise woman in the Sleeping
Beauty fairy tale, originally "Little Briar Rose," recorded
by the Brothers Grimm

UROPHOBIA

Many people have had the occasional encounter with shy-bladder syndrome, as urophobia is sometimes called. Perhaps you're at a ballgame or the movies, and you feel the urge. You get up, go into a public restroom, and then . . . nothing. You want to go, but you can't. What gives?

Urophobia (the Greek word for "urine" is *ouro*) is a kind of social phobia—it arises when people become overly concerned about what others will think of them while they're doing their business (and, yes, there is a fear of defecation, called coprophobia). In essence, when the moment to pee arrives, a person becomes self-conscious and can't relax enough to urinate. They may worry about the sound—Is it a wimpy trickle? A flood?—or the smell (Can anyone tell I just ate asparagus?). Also, it occurs far more frequently in men than women—perhaps because men are often forced to pee at urinals standing side by side with other men.

For most people, this is a rare occurrence. But for some it becomes a chronic problem affecting their everyday lives. Their home bathrooms become their only safe place to pee, which puts a real damper on their social and work lives. Someone with urophobia may not drink enough fluids for fear that they will have to pee in public, or they will hold it for hours on end. In severe cases, they can't even go at home if someone else is present. While this problem may sound funny, it's no joke for the 17 million Americans who can't pee in public.

Urophobia can arise suddenly and unexpectedly for no apparent reason, but for most people, it is triggered by some unpleasant experience—often in the teenage years. One common cause is when a teenager is teased or harassed in the school bathroom. Pretty soon, the bathroom becomes a trigger for anxiety, which in turn switches on that old fight-or-flight response. This anxious reaction makes it pretty much impossible to relax enough to pee.

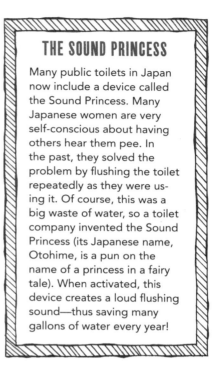

THE SOUND PRINCESS

Many public toilets in Japan now include a device called the Sound Princess. Many Japanese women are very self-conscious about having others hear them pee. In the past, they solved the problem by flushing the toilet repeatedly as they were using it. Of course, this was a big waste of water, so a toilet company invented the Sound Princess (its Japanese name, Otohime, is a pun on the name of a princess in a fairy tale). When activated, this device creates a loud flushing sound—thus saving many gallons of water every year!

Another frequent culprit is when we are asked to pee on demand when faced with the pee-in-the-cup routine at the doctor's office. This can be intimidating for anyone, but it has also been known to trigger long-lasting cases of urophobia.

OVERCOMING THE FEAR

If you can pee in private but not in public, then your problem is probably urophobia. Still, if an inability to pee is a regular issue, you should probably see a medical doctor to make sure that you don't have a physical problem.

Many people with urophobia find that therapy helps give their shy bladder more confidence. There are also some things you can try yourself. The key to these practice sessions is to drink plenty of fluids beforehand. After all, your bladder needs something to work with.

1. While using the toilet at home, where you feel safe, practice whatever relaxation techniques work best for you (for more, see "Overcoming the Fear," page 199). Now, imagine that you are in a public restroom. Stay relaxed as you continue peeing. Repeat several times, or until this seems easy.

2. Next, make a list of restrooms that make you anxious. Rank them from least to most threatening. Perhaps the least threatening is the bathroom in your best friend's house, while the worst is the school bathroom during lunch period. Focus on using "easy" restrooms for a week, and practice those relaxation techniques while you're peeing. Don't *think* about peeing, just let your mind wander and do it. Then, progressively use more difficult restrooms.

3. Meanwhile, get a trusted friend to help you. No, really. If your friend is really a friend, they'll understand. At first, have your friend wait outside the bathroom door while you pee. As you become more comfortable, have your friend join you in the bathroom—they don't have to look. Just put them in another stall or in the shower. If this cracks you both up, all the better—laughter is a great way to relieve anxiety.

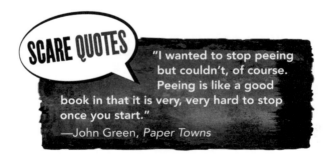

SCARE QUOTES

"I wanted to stop peeing but couldn't, of course. Peeing is like a good book in that it is very, very hard to stop once you start."
—John Green, *Paper Towns*

WICCAPHOBIA

FEAR OF WITCHES

The fear of witches and witchcraft dates back thousands of years. At times, wiccaphobia has been so strong that it has inspired mass hysteria across entire communities, such as during the late-seventeenth-century Salem witch trials. Magic, the supernatural, and the devil's presence were once considered part of everyday reality, and witches were thought to manipulate the supernatural for evil purposes or to serve the devil. The supernatural was blamed for anything bad that happened in a community, and suspected witches were an easy target. Christians believed that God was the source of everything good, and that Satan was responsible for everything bad that happened. And in the Middle Ages, *lots* of bad things happened: plagues, wars, you name it. Clearly, Satan was a busy devil, and witches were his earthly helpers. Did your cow die? Ah, it must have been the witch! Did your crops fail? Burn the witch!

People who used herbs and spells to cure sickness, who defied the teachings of the church, or who seemed to be peculiar were often accused of witchcraft. From the Inquisition in the fourteenth century through the witch trials of the seventeenth century, suspected witches were hanged, drowned, and burned at the stake.

WHO'S WHO: FAMOUS (SOME POSSIBLY REAL) WITCHES THROUGHOUT HISTORY

➡ **Morgan le Fay** (sometimes known as Morgaine) was a powerful sorceress in the King Arthur legends. She was King Arthur's half-sister, and, as "le Fay" (French for "fairy") implies, she was also half-fairy. Most Arthurian legends cast her as a seductive villainess bent on doing in King Arthur. For a more sympathetic view of Morgaine, read Marion Zimmer Bradley's excellent novel *The Mists of Avalon*.

➡ **Moll Dyer** (? – 1697) Moll Dyer, an herbal healer, was a legendary resident of Leonardtown, Maryland. She was said to have been accused of witchcraft and chased out of her home on a bitterly cold winter night. Her body was found a few days later, her hand frozen to a large rock nearby that allegedly bore her handprint for many years. Folklore has it that her spirit continues to haunt the nearby land. The movie *The Blair Witch Project* is rumored to have been based on the Moll Dyer legend.

➡ **Marie Laveau** (1794 – 1881). Marie Laveau, aka the "Voodoo Queen," was a free Creole of color from New Orleans. Her brand of Voodoo combined her Roman Catholic and traditional West African religious beliefs. Along with her daughter, also named Marie Laveau, she developed a huge following and was quite influential. She presided over supposedly blood-drenched rituals involving chicken sacrifices and danced with a snake named Zombi wrapped around her body. People still visit the crypt in a New Orleans cemetery where she was reportedly buried and draw "XXX" on the side, hoping that her spirit will grant them their wishes.

Today, wiccaphobia—the term is from the Old English word *wicca*, meaning a male witch; a female witch was *wicce*—doesn't carry the power it once did; belief in the supernatural and the devil is not what it once was. However, self-identified witches do have a real cultural presence today: They are the self-identified followers of Wicca, a nature-based religion that worships a god and goddess, not Satan. As a group, Wiccans are no more wicked than any other bunch of people. Although a recent survey estimates that 700,000 people consider themselves Wiccans or Pagans (a broad group of people who believe in some sort of earth-based spirituality), fear and distrust of witches remains in the culture and occasionally bubbles up.

It is basic human nature to fear that which we do not understand or to distrust those who we perceive to be somehow different. Unlike prejudice or xenophobia (see page 18), though, wiccaphobia is not driven by hatred of the other, but by a deeply rooted fear of evil. Even if we no longer believe that witches can cause our cows to stop giving milk, for many people they continue to symbolize the things that threaten us. Wiccaphobia may be more of a problem for contemporary witches (or for those accused of witchcraft) than for wiccaphobes themselves. Certain religions continue to teach that demons are real, and that witches do indeed have the power to cast spells. Some Christians feel that the Harry Potter books promote witchcraft, and called for bans on the books in schools and libraries. It is not uncommon for witches to experience discrimination, and in some parts of the world, it is not uncommon for older women to be accused of witchcraft. The Tanzania Legal and Human Rights Center, for example, said that between 2004 and 2009, more than 2,585 older women were killed because they were said to be witches.

If you truly fear witches to the point where it's a problem, you might want to consider the root of your fear. Does your church teach you that witchcraft is evil? Do you believe that they might do you harm? Or is it just that they seem, well, strange? You might try talking with a therapist or spiritual advisor about your fear. Do some research on Wicca or other pagan religions, and try to remain open-minded.

197

SCARE QUOTES

"When, however, one reads of a witch being ducked, of a woman possessed by devils, of a wise woman selling herbs, or even of a very remarkable man who had a mother, then I think we are on the track of a lost novelist, a suppressed poet, of some mute and inglorious Jane Austen, some Emily Brönte who dashed her brains out on the moor or mopped and mowed about the highways crazed with the torture that her gift had put her to."

—Virginia Woolf, *A Room of One's Own*

"'Tis now the very witching time of night; When churchyards yawn and hell itself breathes out Contagion to this world."

—William Shakespeare, *Macbeth*

"When I was a child there were many witches, and they bewitched both cattle and men, especially children."

—Martin Luther

"Fear of serious injury alone cannot justify oppression of free speech and assembly. Men feared witches and burnt women. It is the function of speech to free men from the bondage of irrational fears."

—Louis D. Brandeis, associate justice on the US Supreme Court, 1916–39

APPENDIX: OVERCOMING THE FEAR

"Change your thoughts and you change your world."
—Norman Vincent Peale

DEALING WITH PHOBIAS

I f you have a phobia or a panic disorder, first of all, know that you are not alone. As much as possible, try not to let the fact that you have a specific fear become a further source of worry. The good news is that phobias are highly treatable. Studies show that treatment is successful for as many as 90 percent of anxiety disorders; most people can see improvement within months, weeks, or sometimes even days. And if you deal with a phobia early on, you can prevent it from becoming more serious. Sometimes it's possible for people to overcome their phobias, especially object-specific phobias, on their own. Other phobias, including social phobias or more general anxiety disorders, often require professional help to overcome. However, seeking help is never wrong. Make sure loved ones and family members know what's going on, then enlist their help for dealing with the fear and perhaps also get the help and advice of a trained therapist.

Remember: Not all phobias are created equal. Some are much easier to manage than others. Sometimes it's relatively easy to avoid what you fear, and the impact on your life may be minimal. Someone may have a morbid fear of sharks, but if they live far from the ocean and don't swim anyway, then the fear may rarely come up. When deciding what to do, consider to what degree the phobia interferes with your daily life: Do you experience it daily, weekly, monthly, or less often? Does it cause a lot of worry simply to have it? Does it keep you from doing things you'd otherwise want or need to do? And/or do your feelings of panic or anxiety seem serious enough that they might be endangering your health? If you answer yes, or are not sure, seek the advice of a professional therapist.

Here are some of the techniques that therapists use to help their clients overcome their fears. You can try these on your own or with the help and guidance of someone else.

SYSTEMATIC DESENSITIZATION THERAPY

Maybe you've heard of Pavlov and his drooling dogs. Ivan Pavlov, who was studying the digestive systems of dogs, knew that dogs drooled in anticipation whenever they saw or smelled food. Then he noticed that the dogs also began drooling whenever they saw anyone wearing a lab coat. It turned out that the people who fed the dogs always wore lab coats, so every time the pooches saw a lab coat, they were convinced that food was on its way. Pavlov decided to test this conditioning, and he found that any stimulus, such as the sound of a bell, could, over time, trigger the drool reflex in dogs. Ding-dong: Alpo time!

Just about everyone has had the experience of being classically conditioned. When you were a kid, did you learn that tinkly, happy music outside your door in the summertime meant the arrival of the ice cream truck—and a delicious treat? Does the sound of an ice cream truck today get your mouth watering? That's a typical example of classical conditioning.

What does this have to do with treating phobias? Systematic desensitization therapy works on the same principle. Through conditioning, it creates a positive association where we now have a negative one. Then, when we are faced with something scary (like speaking in public, for example), we learn to replace our feelings of anxiety and panic with calm and relaxation.

Step Number One: Relax!

You may think you know how to relax: kick off your shoes, lie on the sofa, and watch reruns of your favorite TV show. That's one way to unwind. But relaxation techniques teach you how to switch on those calm feelings anytime, anywhere, and when you really need them—whenever anxiety takes over.

Here are some relaxation tips. Experiment to see what works best for you, and practice for a few minutes every day, until you can easily put yourself into a relaxed state when you want.

1. "Breathe deep, seek peace." This was a common greeting in the book *Dinotopia: A Land Apart from Time*, by James Gurney, but it's a great mantra for calming down. When people are anxious, they tend to take rapid, shallow breaths. This just makes things worse. Practice taking slow, deep breaths: put your hand on your stomach, and count to three as you inhale from deep within your belly. Count to three again as you exhale completely. Feel your belly rise and fall with each breath. Put other thoughts out of your mind and focus only on your breath. You might try saying "ah" to yourself as you inhale and "so" as you exhale. Experiment and see what works for you.

2. When we are anxious, that fight-or-flight instinct makes us tense up. Try this: clench your jaw—a common anxiety response. Next, release and relax those same muscles. Feel the way your throat opens up, unclench your teeth, and remove your tongue from the top of your mouth. Practice clenching and relaxing different muscles.

3. Close your eyes and think of a place that you find especially peaceful. Use all of your senses to explore this special place. If you think of sitting beside a quiet brook, for example, you might see the sunlight sparkling on the water. Listen to the sound of the water splashing over the rocks. Imagine putting your bare feet in the brook and feel the water wash over them. Enjoy that feeling of relaxation, and keep it with you as you open your eyes.

Step Number Two: Rank Your Fears

Make a list of situations related to your phobia and rank them, giving the scariest situation a score of 100 and the least scary a score of 5. Try to come up with at least ten to twenty situations that are fairly evenly scattered along the scale. Write them down on index cards, then arrange them in order, from least to most scary.

Let's say you have a great singing voice, and you'd love to play the lead in the school musical, but you experience a wave of topophobia (performance anxiety, page 182) whenever you try to sing in public. You might give singing in the shower a ranking of 5, while singing karaoke at home with a group of friends might merit a 50. Is singing in front of a packed auditorium the worst thing you can think of? Give it a 100.

Step Number Three: Face Your Fears

Get into a comfortable position and practice some relaxation techniques. Once you're good and mellow, pick up the lowest-ranked card. Close your eyes and imagine yourself in that situation for a few seconds; if you feel anxiety creep in, just focus again on your relaxation practice till you're calm. After a couple of minutes, pick up the same card and again imagine the scenario. Still feeling mellow? Great! Pick up the next card and do the same thing, moving progressively through more difficult situations. It may take a few sessions, maybe even a lot of sessions, to work through the entire scale of fears. Don't worry how long it takes. Any progress is good progress.

Here's another example of how it works. Say you suffer from cynophobia, or fear of dogs. While you find puppies no big deal, breeds that are known to be aggressive freak you out. So, your first card might be thinking of the cutest puppy in the world. Then, you might picture an older dog snoozing, then a dog chasing a ball, then you feeding a large dog. If you can stay in your mellow place with each one, continue imagining more difficult scenarios: say, a small dog barking excitedly, then a larger dog doing the same thing, and so on. At each point, don't move on until you can imagine the scene and still remain relaxed and calm.

However, as you feel more comfortable, consider facing your fears in real life, if possible, using your relaxation techniques to help you stay calm. For some fears, like with dogs, this is relatively easy to do in a controlled way. If you have friends with well-behaved, friendly dogs, ask for their help. Arrange a meeting. Then, while your friend holds the dog on leash, let the dog approach you—say, while you're sitting on a sofa or a park bench. Don't talk to the dog or touch it. Just let it sniff you while you practice your relaxation techniques. If you can stay calm, continue the interaction. Let the dog lick your hand, or pet it gently. Then, stop the session while you're still feeling relaxed, and try to pick up the next session at the same point. Soon, you may have a new canine friend, as well as the confidence that you can manage your anxiety in other scenarios.

COGNITIVE BEHAVIORAL THERAPY

Many professional therapists today also use cognitive behavioral therapy (CBT) to treat phobias and other anxiety disorders. This approach focuses on changing those thought patterns that make us anxious. You may think that you have no control over the anxious thoughts that fly around in your head. CBT teaches us that we *are* in control.

Let's take that phobia about singing in public. What, exactly, are you afraid of? Is it that your voice will crack, or that you will forget the words? Do you fear the idea of people laughing at you? Make a list of every thought or fear related to your phobia. Now, for each item on the list, write out the answers to these three questions:

1. What evidence do I have that this is actually true? Is it likely that you will forget the words to a song that you have rehearsed countless times?

2. How could things go differently than you fear? Perhaps that you remember every single word to your song and belt it out, giving the performance of your life.

3. If what you fear occurs, what would happen? If you forgot some words, you could hum or scat nonsense until you got your bearings. This happens to seasoned performers all the time. Ella Fitzgerald, one of the greatest jazz singers of all time, famously forgot the words to "Mack the Knife" halfway through the song and made up the rest. The performance was unforgettable.

One characteristic of phobias is that they are exaggerated fears that overestimate the actual danger. By evaluating these fears, you can replace any irrational negative expectations with more positive, reasonable ones. That is the "cognitive" part of CBT. The "behavioral" part of the therapy is similar to systematic desensitization therapy: it uses the same techniques of relaxation and gradual exposure to the things that make us fearful.

Here's an example of the way CBT works: let's say someone suffers from arachnophobia, or fear of spiders, and tarantulas really creep them out. Still with us? At the beginning of the session, a therapist might show the person pictures of a tarantula while talking about what we know about them. That they can't jump. That they rarely bite, and if they do, their venom is weaker than a bee's. That they are shy and fragile creatures who try to protect themselves first. That they play an important role in nature by preying on insects and other small creatures.

As this education continues, the therapist might introduce a live tarantula in a closed terrarium. Eventually, the person would move closer and touch the wall of the terrarium. If this went well, and the person still felt relaxed, they would touch the tarantula itself, first with a paintbrush and then with their hands.

The remarkable thing about this type of treatment is that over the course of about two or three hours, you can actually change the wiring in your brain. You train yourself not to fear.

However, it should also be said that overcoming phobias is rarely as easy as this may make it sound. If they were easy to get rid of, they wouldn't be phobias. This is why it's important to seek out professional help. In some cases, a therapist may suggest medication to help manage your anxiety. While medications aren't usually considered a long-term option to treat phobias, they can keep symptoms under control while you work with your therapist. If you do take any type of medication, make sure that you take it exactly as prescribed, and always under the supervision of a licensed professional.

Support groups can also be very helpful, especially ones for teens with similar anxiety problems. It can be very comforting to know that other kids have some of the same fears and anxieties you do.

RESOURCES

Websites

Anxiety and Depression Association of America (www.adaa.org): ADAA is a nonprofit association dedicated to the prevention, treatment, and cure of anxiety, depression, and related disorders and to improving the lives of all people who suffer from them.

American Psychological Association: Anxiety (www.apa.org/topics/anxiety): This site contains a comprehensive section on anxiety disorders, with full access to the APA's online publication *Monitor on Psychology.*

National Institute of Mental Health: Anxiety Disorders (www.nimh.nih.gov/health/topics/anxiety-disorders): This government-run institute provides another comprehensive resource on anxiety disorders.

Books

Korgeski, Gregory P. *The Complete Idiot's Guide to Phobias.* New York: Alpha, 2009.

Saul, Helen. *Phobias: Fighting the Fear.* New York: HarperCollins, 2001.

Schab, Lisa M. *The Anxiety Workbook for Teens: Activities to Help You Deal with Anxiety and Worry.* Oakland, CA: Instant Help, 2008.

NOTES

Page 14, Introduction: Phobias 101

Scientists have found that the connection between the prefrontal cortex: M. Justin Kim, et al, "The Structural and Functional Connectivity of the Amygdala: From Normal Emotion to Pathological Anxiety," *Behavioral Brain Research* 223 (2011): 403–410.

This might explain why anxiety disorders seem to spike during or just before adolescence: Siobhan S. Pattwell, et al, "Altered Fear Learning Across Development in Both Mouse and Human," *Proceedings of the National Academy of Sciences (PNAS),* September 17, 2012 (early online edition).

Nearly one in three teens suffers from some sort of anxiety disorder: Kathleen Ries Merikangas, et al, "Lifetime Prevalence of Mental Disorders in US Adolescents: Results from the National Comorbidity Study—Adolescent Supplement (NCS-A)," *Journal of the American Academy of Child and Adolescent Psychiatry* 49, no. 10 (October 2010): 980–989.

Page 22, Acrophobia: Fear of Heights

One scientific study found babies would refuse to crawl across a sturdy: E. J. Gibson & R. D. Walk, "The Visual Cliff," *Scientific American* 202, no. 4 (1960): 67–71.

Page 26, Agoraphobia: Fear of Public or Open Spaces

According to the National Institute of Mental Health, about 1.8 million Americans: http://www.nimh.nih.gov/health/publications/the-numbers-count-mental-disorders-in-america/index.shtml#Agoraphobia.

"I'm just from meeting, Susie, and as I sorely feared": Maryanne Garbowski, *The House Without the Door: A Study of Emily Dickinson and the Illness of Agoraphobia* (Madison, NJ: Farleigh Dickinson University Press, 1989), 34–35.

"I was out walking with two friends—the sun began to set": Ulrich Bischoff, *Edvard Munch and the Physiology of Symbolism* (Cranbury, NJ: Rosemont, 2002), 29.

Page 30, Ailurophobia: Fear of Cats

Consequently, rats spread the microbe that caused the Black Death, a plague: Gloria Stephens, *Legacy of the Cat* (San Francisco: Chronicle Books, 2001), 8.

Legend has it that one of the greatest military leaders in history, Napoleon Bonaparte: Carl Van Vechten, *The Tiger in the House,* chapter 3: "Ailurophobes and Other Cat Haters," 1922. http://www.bartleby.com/234/3.html#txt1.

Page 33, Aquaphobia: Fear of Water

Natalie's fear was tragically justified; in 1981, the then-forty-three-year-old actress: http://www.ibtimes.com/natalie-woods-death-case-reveals-lifelong-eerie-connection-water-372322.

Page 36, Arachnophobia: Fear of Spiders

Not all cultures have a built-in fear of spiders. In Brazil, for example: Helen Saul, *Phobias: Fighting the Fear* (New York: HarperCollins, 2011), 84–85.

Interestingly, and to make matters worse, studies have shown that people who are afraid of spiders: Michael W. Vasey, et al, "It Was as Big as My Head, I Swear!" *Journal of Anxiety Disorders* 26, no. 1 (January 2012): 20–24.

After the therapy—those parts of your brain stay relatively quiet when faced with a spider: Katherina K. Hauner, et al, "Exposure Therapy Triggers Lasting Reorganization of Neural Fear Processing." *Proceedings of the National Academy of Sciences* 109, no. 23 (June 5, 2012): 9203–9208.

As one study put it, "Change the mind and you change the brain": Vincent Paquette, et al, "'Change the Mind and You Change the Brain': Effects of Cognitive-Behavioral Therapy on the Neural Correlates of Spider Phobia," *NeuroImage* 18 (2003): 401–409.

Page 40, Astraphobia: Fear of Thunderstorms

Scientists estimate that nearly 9 percent of people will have a storm phobia: G. C. Curtis, W. J. Magee, W. W. Eaton, et al, "Specific Fears and Phobias. Epidemiology and Classification," *British Journal of Psychiatry* 173 (1993): 213.

Page 44, Ataxophobia: Fear of Disorder

His wife, Victoria (aka Posh Spice) once told an interviewer: Maxine Frith, "Beckham Reveals His Battle with Obsessive Disorder," *Independent*, Monday, April 3, 2006. http://www.independent.co.uk/news/uk/this-britain/beckham-reveals-his-battle-with-obsessive-disorder-472573.html.

David himself has said, "Walk into a hotel room and before I can get settled": Alex Bilmes, "David Beckham: Not on the Team, Still in the Game," *Esquire (UK)*, September 2012.

Page 47, Aviophobia: Fear of Flying

In fact, one-third to one-half of people who fear flying say: "Fear of flying: Learning to fly comfortably," Anxiety and Stress Disorders Institute. http://www.anxietyandstress.com/fearofflying.html.

White has gone public about the need for the NBA to address mental health issues: "Royce White: Speaking Out, Fighting Stigma," Anxiety and Depression Association of America. http://adaa.org/living-with-anxiety/personal-stories/royce-white.

Page 50, Botanophobia: Fear of Plants

An older superstition may actually have led to this idea. People once thought: Richard Webster, *The Encyclopedia of Superstitions* (Woodbury, MN: Llewellyn Worldwide, 2008), 106.

Actress Christina Ricci told Esquire magazine in 2003 that she has a phobia about houseplants: Tim Lewis, "Christina Ricci Is Not Crazy," *Esquire*, July 2003.

Page 53, Chiroptophobia: Fear of Bats

Like any wild animal, bats can carry rabies, but less than 1 percent of bats have rabies: Brandon J. Klug, Amy S. Turmelle, James A. Ellison, Erin F. Baerwald, and Robert M. R. Barclay, "Rabies Prevalence in Migratory Tree-Bats in Alberta and the Influence of Roosting Ecology and Sampling Method on Reported Prevalence of Rabies in Bats," *Journal of Wildlife Disease* 47 (2011): 64–77.

Like cats, European medieval folklore associated bats with witches: Richard Webster, *The Encyclopedia of Superstitions* (Woodbury, MN: Llewellyn Worldwide, 2008), 24.

The ancient Mayans, for example, worshipped a vampire bat god called Camazotz: Elizabeth P. Benson, "Bats in South American Folklore and Ancient Art," *Bats Magazine* 9, no. 1 (Spring 1991). http://www.batcon.org/index.php/media-and-info/bats-archives.html?task=viewArticle&magArticleID=477.

Page 57, Claustrophobia: Fear of Confined Spaces

At least one in ten people admits to being at least mildly phobic: S. J. Rachman, "Claustrophobia," in *Phobias: A Handbook of Theory, Research, and Treatment,* Graham C. L. Favey, ed. (Hobokenn, NJ: Wiley, 1997), 165.

Researchers believe this based on an ancient fear of being trapped: Rush W. Dozier Jr., *Fear Itself: The Origin and Nature of the Powerful Emotion That Shapes Our Lives and Our World* (New York: St. Martin's, 1998), 103.

Scientists have found that the amygdalae (where we experience fear in the brain): A. E. Ziemann, et al, "The Amygdala Is a Chemosensor That Detects Carbon Dioxide and Acidosis to Elicit Fear Behavior," *Cell* 139 (2009): 1012–1020.

Page 60, Coulrophobia: Fear of Clowns

In fact, when a British university conducted a poll to improve the décor: Finlo Rohrer, "Why are clowns scary?" *BBC News Magazine,* January 16, 2008. http://news.bbc.co.uk/2/hi/uk_news/magazine/7191721.stm.

The term coulrophobia derives from the Greek word kolobatheron, for "stilt": Oxford Dictionary. http://oxforddictionaries.com/definition/american_english/coulrophobia?region=us&q=coulrophobia.

Paul Salkovskis, an expert in anxiety disorders, told the BBC in 2008 that things: Finlo Rohrer, "Why Are Clowns Scary?" *BBC News Magazine,* 16 January 2008. http://news.bbc.co.uk/2/hi/uk_news/magazine/7191721.stm.

In a 2010 interview with National Public Radio's Michele Norris, Paul Carpenter: "Clowns Teach People Not to be Afraid of . . . Clowns," National Public Radio, June 17, 2010. http://www.npr.org/templates/story/story.php?storyId=127911469.

"I also have had an acute fear of clowns—a condition known as coulrophobia": "Celebrities Reveal Their Deepest Fears," *Courier Mail,* July 7, 2008. http://www.couriermail.com.au/news/phobias-of-rich-and-famous/story-e6freon6-1111116845139.

Page 67, Dentophobia: Fear of Dentists

Up to 80 percent of adults in the United States admit to having some anxieties: The Encyclopedia of Phobias, Fears, and Anxieties, 2nd Ed., Ronald M. Doctor and Ada P. Kahn, eds. (New York: Facts on File, Inc., 2000), 170.

There are nearly as many reasons people fear going to the dentist as there are teeth in the mouth: D. Locker, D. Shapiro, and A. Liddell, "Negative Dental Experiences and Their Relationship to Dental Anxiety," *Community Dental Health* 13, no. 2 (June 1996): 86–92.

some psychologists believe that the disorder is actually closer to post-traumatic stress disorder: H. Stefan Bracha, et al, "Post-traumatic Dental-Care Anxiety (PTDA): Is "Dental Phobia" a Misnomer?" *Hawaii Dental Journal* (September/October 2006): 17–19.

In 1841, Lincoln went to a dentist to have a tooth extracted: "To Miss Mary Speed—Practical Slavery, " from *The Writings of Abraham Lincoln,* Vol. 1. http://www.classicreader.com/book/3237/37.

According to one account, he "took a container of chloroform": John R. Bumgarner, *The Health of the Presidents: The 41 United States Presidents Through 1993 from a Physician's Point of View* (Jefferson, NC: MacFarland & Co., 1994), 95.

Page 75, Entomophobia: Fear of Insects

scientists estimate that, at any one time, there are nearly 10 quintillion insects in the world: Entomological Society of America. Frequently Asked Questions on Entomology. http://www.entsoc.org/resources/faq/#triv1.

Put another way, for every pound of human there are about two hundred pounds of insects: Natalie Angier, "A Large-Size Focus on Life Lived Small," *New York Times* (January 5, 2009). http://www.nytimes.com/2009/01/06/science/06angi.html?_r=0.

"I jump out of planes, I could be covered in cockroaches, I do all sorts of things": "Kidman's Butterfly Fears." http://www.imdb.com/news/ni0061663.

"Nothing seems to please a fly so much as to be mistaken for a huckleberry": Puck, 1877, Vols. 1–2, p. 13. Free e-book.

Page 80, Equinophobia: Fear of Horses

Kansas City Chiefs safety Eric Berry is fearless when it comes to facing his opponents: Chuck Schilken, "Eric Berry's Fear of Horses Follows Him to Football Field," *Los Angeles Times.* http://articles.latimes.com/2012/nov/15/sports/la-sp-sn-eric-berry-horses-20121115.

Actress Kristen Stewart had to overcome her intense fear of horses for her role: Jessica Wedmeyer, "Kristen Stewart Confronts Her Fear—of Horses," *People Pets* (March 20, 2012). http://www.peoplepets.com/people/pets/article/0,,20579708,00.html.

psychiatrists today make a convincing argument that Freud's interpretation of the case was not accurate: Joseph Wolpe and Stanley Rachmann, "A Little Child Shall Mislead Them." In *Unauthorized Freud: Doubters Confront a Legend* (New York: Viking, 1998).

Page 83, Gephyrophobia: Fear of Bridges

Every year, a service in Maryland drives about four thousand people over the Chesapeake Bay Bridge: http://usatoday30.usatoday.com/news/health/2007-08-07-bridge-phobia-sidebar_N.htm.

Page 85, Hemophobia: Fear of Blood

experts say that nearly 15 percent of us have passed out at the sight of blood at some point: Stephanie Watson, "Swoon at the Sight of Blood? Why the Sight of Blood Might Make You Faint—and What You Can Do About It," *WebMD Magazine.* http://www.webmd.com/mental-health/features/swoon-at-the-sight-of-blood.

Page 88, Kakorraphiaphobia: Fear of Failure

"I didn't see it then, but it turned out that getting fired from Apple": http://www.huffingtonpost.com/2011/10/05/steve-jobs-stanford-commencement-address_n_997301.html.

Page 92, Kinemortophobia: Fear of Zombies

In some descriptions, if a person dies an unnatural death: http://www.umich.edu/~uncanny/zombies.html.

Page 96, Koumpounophobia: Fear of Buttons

One British bartender whose aspirations of becoming an accountant were dashed: Steve White, "Terrified of Buttons for 20 years: Dad Could Not Wear a Shirt Because the Buttons Made Him Sick," *Mirror* (April 27, 2012). http://www.mirror.co.uk/news/uk-news/terrified-of-buttons-for-20-years-dad-807903.

Page 100, Musophobia: Fear of Mice or Rats

Disney was actually very fond of mice. When he was a young artist: J. Michael Barrier, *The Animated Man: A Life of Walt Disney* (Berkeley: University of California Press, 2007), 56.

That myth dates all the way back to the first century AD, when Pliny the Elder wrote: Pliny's Natural History, Vol. 1–3, p 15. Free eBook.

Page 104, Mysophobia: Fear of Germs

Katherine Ashenburg, the author of The Dirt on Clean: An Unsanitized History, *says:* http://www.salon.com/2007/11/30/dirt_on_clean/.

Perhaps the world's most famous mysophobe was Howard Hughes, an American aviator: M. Dittmann, "Hughes's Germ Phobia Revealed in Psychological Autopsy," *Monitor on Psychology* 36, no. 7(July 2005): 102. http://www.apa.org/monitor/julaug05/hughes.aspx.

"Personally I never take any precautions against germs": http://www.youtube.com/watch?v=CnmMNdiCz_s.

Page 112, Nomophobia: Fear of Being Out of Mobile Phone Contact

According to these researchers, about two-thirds of the British public are nomophobic: http://www.securenvoy.com/blog/2012/02/16/66-of-the-population-suffer-from-nomophobia-the-fear-of-being-without-their-phone.

Another survey found that 22 percent of people would rather give up their toothbrush: Danielle Braff, "Being Glued to Your Cell is a Problem, Experts Say," *Chicago Tribune* (January 18, 2012). http://articles.chicagotribune.com/2012-01-18/health/sc-health-0118-cell-phone-20120118_1_internet-addiction-iphone-users-slot-machines.

Page 115, Nosocomephobia: Fear of Hospitals

One recent study found that one-third of hospital patients: Kevin B. O'Reilley, "1 in 3 Patients Harmed During Hospital Stay." http://www.amednews.com/article/20110418/profession/304189940/2.

"If I go into the hospital, I'll never come out alive.": "Nixon Rejecting Care in Hospital," *Spokane Daily Chronicle* (September 16, 1974). http://news.google.com/newspapers?id=lqsSAAAAIBAJ&sjid=WPgDAAAAIBAJ&pg=4515,241547&dq=fear+of+hospital&hl=en.

Page 121, Obesophobia: Fear of Becoming Fat

"Even when someone gets to looking like she should be so proud of herself": http://omg.yahoo.com/blogs/balancedliving/melissa-mccarthy-her-weight-struggle-sometimes-wish-were-194954203.html.

"I enjoy being me; I always have done. I've seen people where it rules their lives": http://www.celebitchy.com/178616/adele_covers_vogue_uk_says_her_weight_has_just_never_been_an_issue.

"There would be all kinds of weird challenges to deal with": http://hollywood-life.com/2013/03/14/lena-dunham-weight-victorias-secret-model-body-playboy.

Page 124, Ophidiophobia: Fear of Snakes

Apparently, Matt Damon cried "like a baby and rock[ed] back and forth": http://www.peoplepets.com/people/pets/article/0,,20553257,00.html.

Page 128, Ornithophobia: Fear of Birds

Lucille Ball, the great comedic actress, hated and feared birds: Kathleen Brady, *Lucille: The Life of Lucille Ball* (New York: Random House Digital, 2001), 7.

actress Scarlett Johansson told the New York Post that she is scared of birds: "Scarlett Johansson on Her Fear of Birds," *New York Post* (December 15, 2011). http://www.nypost.com/p/pagesix/scarlett_johansson_on_her_fear_of_eQ3NUYVnIQ3NIpiAmpmnpN.

But she said recently, "I really like birds. Everyone always wants me to say": John Hiscock, "Tippi Hedren Interview: 'Hitchcock Put Me in a Mental Prison,'" *The Telegraph* (December 24, 2012). http://www.telegraph.co.uk/culture/film/starsandstories/9753977/Tippi-Hedren-interview-Hitchcock-put-me-in-a-mental-prison.html.

Page 136, Pediophobia: Fear of Dolls

Bray said, "You can't look it in the eyes. That's how it gets to you. You can't look it in the eyes": http://www.youtube.com/watch?v=6GRtNvvef08.

Page 145, Pyrophobia: Fear of Fire

Hans Christian Andersen became pyrophobic after a good friend died in a fire on board: Helen Saul, *Phobias: Fighting the Fear* (New York: HarperCollins, 2001), 15.

Page 152, Selachophobia: Fear of Sharks

That all changed in 1916. Bathing in the ocean had only recently become a popular pastime: Richard G. Fernicola, *Twelve Days of Terror: A Definitive Investigation of the 1916 New Jersey Shark Attacks* (Guilford, CT: Lyons Press, 2002).

"You always hear a headline like this: 'Man Killed by Shark.'": Reporters' Notebook/Bits & Pieces of News…, *Buffalo News.com* (August 30, 2012). http://www.buffalonews.com/apps/pbcs.dll/article?AID=/20120830/CITYANDREGION/120839757&template=printart.

Page 156, Sinistrophobia: Fear of Using the Left Hand

An ancient Greek philosopher once wrote, "The starting point is honorable": "Right and Left in Greek Philosophy," Lloyd, G. E. R., *Journal of Hellenic Studies* 82 (1962): 61–2.

"The left half of the brain is dominant in right-handed people": Dennis L. Molfese and Sidney J. Segalowitz, *Brain Lateralization in Children: Developmental Implications"* (New York: Guilford Press, 1988): 220.

"When I was a kid I seemed to do everything from back to front": Melissa Roth, *The Left Stuff: How the Left-Handed Have Survived and Thrived in a Right-Handed World* (Boulder, CO: Evans, 2005), 37.

"I think left-handed people tend to have a chip on their shoulder": Melissa Roth, *The Left Stuff: How the Left-Handed Have Survived and Thrived in a Right-Handed World* (Boulder, CO: Evans, 2005), 183.

Page 160, Social Phobia: Social Anxiety Disorder

Charles Darwin noticed this all the way back in 1872, when he quoted a physician: Eric Hollander and Nicholas Bakalar, *Coping with Social Anxiety: The Definitive Guide to Effective Treatment Options* (New York: Henry Holt, 2005), 7.

Recently, scientists have found that people with social anxiety seem to be genetically programmed: http://psychcentral.com/news/2008/03/04/genetic-disposition-for-anxiety/1997.html.

Former football player Ricky Williams had always considered himself shy: http://www.adaa.org/living-with-anxiety/personal-stories/ricky-williams-story-social-anxiety-disorder.

Page 169, Spectrophobia: Fear of Mirrors

One Bloody Mary legend says that she lived in Massachusetts in the seventeenth century: Linda S. Watts, *Encyclopedia of American Folklore* (New York: Infobase Publishing, 2006), 41.

In one experiment, participants reported seeing their own faces: Giovanni B. Caputo, "Strange-face-in-the-mirror illusion," *Perception* 39 (2010): 1007–1008.

Page 173, Swinophobia: Fear of Pigs

When a pig escaped on the set of Kingdom of Heaven, *actor Orlando Bloom:* http://www.usmagazine.com/entertainment/pictures/stars-weird-phobias-2011211/18198.

Page 175, Taphophobia: Fear of Being Buried Alive

According to the story, she walked to her house and rang the doorbell: Franz Hartmann, *Buried Alive: An Examination into the Occult Causes of Apparent Death, Trance, and Catalepsy* (Boston Occult Publishing, 1895), 17.

But the gold standard for determining death was just to wait a few days: Mary Roach, *Stiff: The Curious Lives of Human Cadavers* (New York: W.W. Norton, 2003), 171–2.

On his deathbed, George Washington said, "I am just going": "Tobias Lear's Journal Account of George Washington's Last Illness and Death," *The Papers of George Washington.* http://gwpapers.virginia.edu/project/exhibit/mourning/lear.html.

The composer Frédéric Chopin's last words were, "The earth is suffocating": Christine Quigley, *The Corpse: A History* (Jefferson, NC: McFarland, 1996), 187.

Hans Christian Andersen lived in mortal fear of being buried alive: Jan Bondeson, *Buried Alive: The Terrifying History of Our Most Primal Fear* (New York: W.W. Norton, 2001), 231.

Page 178, Thanatophobia: Fear of Death

Scientists have shown that people with phobic anxieties such as the fear of crowded places: Lana L. Watkins, et al, "Prospective association between phobic anxiety and cardiac mortality in individuals with coronary heart disease," *Psychsometric Medicine* 72, no. 7 (September 2010): 664–671.

"It was horrible," Gellar said. "It's really hard to be a vampire slayer": "Buffy the Vampire Slayer: Q&A with Sarah Michelle Gellar." http://www.phase9.tv/moviefeatures/buffythevampireslayerq&a-sarahmichellegellar1.shtml.

In her will, Parker left her estate to Martin Luther King: Nell Greenfield Boyce, "How Dorothy Parker Came to Rest in Baltimore," National Public Radio (June 7, 2012). http://www.npr.org/2012/06/07/154148811/how-dorothy-parker-came-to-rest-in-baltimore.

Page 182, Topophobia: Fear of Performing

Some claim that the fear of public speaking—which is also called glossophobia: http://www.webmd.com/anxiety-panic/guide/20061101/fear-public-speaking.

Singer Carly Simon has struggled with stage fright throughout her career: http://articles.courant.com/1995-03-09/entertainment/9505021583_1_stage-fright-letters-foxwoods-resort-casino.

One time, early in her career, Simon was performing on a small stage: http://www.huffingtonpost.com/carly-simon/bless-you-my-hero_b_150552.html.

"It's amazing. You can look out front of a big crowd—let's say twenty thousand": http://www.oprah.com/oprahshow/Barbra-Streisands-Stage-Fright-Video.

Page 185, Triskaidekaphobia: Fear of the Number Thirteen

Friggatriskaidekaphobia is probably the most common superstition in the United States; according to researchers: John Roach, "Friday the 13th Phobia Rooted in Ancient History," *National Geographic News* (August 12, 2004). http://news.nationalgeographic.com/news/2004/02/0212_040212_friday13. html.

One study published in the British Medical Journal *found that people:* T. J. Scanlon, et al, "Is Friday the 13th Bad for Your Health?" *British Medical Journal* 307 (December 1993): 1584–1586.

Hoover was also known to be triskaidekaphobic; when he was running for president: Nathaniel Lachenmeyer, *13: The Story of the World's Most Popular Superstition* (New York: Thunder's Mouth, 2004), 176–177.

The first person to die in a car accident was killed in New York City on September 13, 1899: http://www.udel.edu/udmessenger/vol17no2/stories/research_ dr13.html.

Page 192, Urophobia: Fear of Urination

While it may sound funny, it's no joke for the 17 million Americans: http:// www.webmd.com/anxiety-panic/features/secret-social-phobia.

Page 195, Wiccaphobia: Fear of Witches

"Fear of serious injury alone cannot justify oppression of free speech and assembly": Scott J. Hammond, Kevin R. Hardwick, and Howard Leslie Lubert, eds., *Classics of American Political and Constitutional Thought: Reconstruction to the Present* (Cambridge, MA: Hackett, 2007), 532.

Page 199, Overcoming the Fear

Studies show that treatment is successful for as many as 90 percent of anxiety disorders: William T. Hey, et al, "Understanding Adolescent Anxiety Disorders: What Teachers, Health Educators, and Practitioners Should Know and Do," *International Electronic Journal of Health Education* 4 (2001): 81–91. http:// www.aahperd.org/aahe/publications/iejhe/upload/01_W_Hey.pdf.

The "behavioral" part of the therapy is similar to systematic desensitization therapy: Allen R. Miller, *Living with Anxiety Disorders* (Farmington Hills, MI: Gale), 32–46.

INDEX

CONTRIBUTORS

Sara L. Latta is a scientist turned science writer. She graduated from the University of Chicago with a Master's degree in Immunology and later earned her MFA in Creative Writing. Her works include *Bones: Dead People DO Tell Tales; The Good, the Bad, the Slimy: The Secret Life of Microbes,* as well as other science books for young people. She lives and works in New York City.

Elizabeth McMahon, PhD, is an award-winning psychologist with over thirty years' experience treating anxiety, panic attacks, phobias, and fears using virtual reality and other proven therapies. In her private practice in San Francisco, she helps people overcome anxiety, reduce stress, increase happiness, and prevent burnout. She has written four books; her next book will be a self-help workbook for people with panic attacks.